RESCUING THE 'INNER CHILD'

HUMAN HORIZONS SERIES

RESCUING THE 'INNER CHILD'

Therapy for Adults Sexually Abused as Children

PENNY PARKS

A CONDOR BOOK
SOUVENIR PRESS (E&A) LTD

First published 1990 by Souvenir Press
(Educational & Academic) Ltd,
43 Great Russell Street, London WC1B 3PA
and simultaneously in Canada

Reprinted 1991

ISBN 0 285 65089 0 paperback
ISBN 0 285 65084 X hardback

Printed in Great Britain by
The Guernsey Press Co. Ltd, Guernsey, Channel Islands.

To Dolly and Angel—
my beloved daughters, cherished friends, kindest critics and
valued supporters—I love you.

To Rod—
my loving husband, loyal and supportive friend, financial backer
and respected adviser—you are the treasure I thought I would
never find.

Contents

Acknowledgements

I would like to thank Elaine Botelho for many hours of typing, Pippa Smyth for help with editing and anglicising, Peter Holden for editing, anglicising and answering queries, and all three for their tireless support.

Most of all, I would like to express my gratitude and respect to those clients who bravely shared their painful childhood experiences with the hope that others might thereby learn how to 'grasp recovery'.

The excerpt on p. 30 is reprinted with permission from *Conspiracy of Silence: The Trauma of Incest,* © 1978, 1985 by Sandra Butler. Published by Volcano Press, Inc. P.O. Box 270, Volcano, CA 95689, USA. (209) 296–3445.

Penny Parks

AUTHOR'S NOTE

Note For ease of reading, victims of sexual abuse will be referred to throughout this book as 'she' rather than 'she/he', but both sexes are abused and the information in this book applies equally. The terms 'abuser' and 'aggressor' will be used interchangeably. The term 'victim' will be used rather than the term 'survivor', for 'victim' simply refers to an innocent person who is or has been subjected to oppression, hardship or mistreatment.

Introduction

When people think of sexual abuse of children, they usually picture a stranger luring a child away with sweets and violently raping and murdering the child. They picture a frantic mother pleading for the safe return of her child, and a newspaper headline of the tragedy. The demand is then made for something to be done about crimes of that nature.

According to statistics published by the National Society for the Prevention of Cruelty to Children, in only 14% of the cases of child sexual abuse is the abuser a stranger to the child: 86% of such crimes are committed by relatives or someone known to the child (S. J. Greighton and P. Noyes, *Child Abuse Trends in England and Wales,* NSPCC, 1989—suspected abuser other than a relative or parent substitute in 14% of sexual-abuse cases from 1983–7). The most common abuser is the natural father. There is no need to lure the child away with sweets—ready access and authority over the child already exist. Although the child does not understand the parent's reasons or actions, she sees no choice but to obey his requests.

Unlike the stranger who violently rapes and usually murders, the family aggressor starts slowly. Normal hugging and cuddling changing to sexual fondling may be the first step. The child is confused and frightened by this new behaviour—wanting the cuddling, but unable to see how to avoid the other unwanted attention. The aggressor capitalises on the child's naïvety and threatens that the child will 'be in trouble', 'go to jail', 'not be loved anymore' or perhaps 'have to go away' if she tells anyone about what *she*—the child—has done.

Children are very susceptible to threats of that kind, and they are easy targets to pin guilt upon—because of their naïvety, they do not understand that they are being tricked. Besides, children commonly experience the problem of guilt by association. For instance, if a child is in the lounge with a friend who accidentally breaks a vase, it is not the friend that her mother shouts at and blames.

The child has no reason not to believe the trusted adult or relative, so the aggressor is free to bribe and blackmail until he feels quite secure that the secret will be kept. If the secret is found out or the child actually tells (which usually does not happen for years—perhaps only when a younger brother or sister is abused by the same parent, or the child reaches puberty) there are no blaring headlines or frantic mother pleading her child's case as there would be if the abuser were a stranger. In fact, until recently society seemed only to recognise children who were molested by strangers—it was too threatening to accept that a child down the street, next door or in someone's own home could be sexually abused by her father.

That abusing father (or relative) could easily be a policeman, a clergyman, a doctor, a lawyer or a member of the armed forces. Although society has seemed to want to categorise child-molesters as alcoholics, unemployed, uneducated, lower-class or criminal types only, in truth aggressors come from *all* walks of life and professions. When the profile of the abuser did not fit what society could tolerate, the abuse was simply justified by blaming the child ('must have been provocative') or the mother ('must have been frigid' etc.). However, to be fair, society often did not find out about such cases, for they were seldom divulged by the child's mother.

The majority of cases brought to a mother's attention by her child were disbelieved. If society did not want to know that fathers sexually abuse their own children, one can imagine how much more difficult it has been for mothers to accept this life-crushing information.

So, here is a crime that was only acknowledged as a crime in 14% of the total number of cases. That is like saying that murder is acknowledged as a crime only when the victim is redheaded. This social quirk made it possible for men (fewer aggressors are female) to sexually abuse children for years and, if found out, generally not have to face any consequences.

Fortunately, a small number of people have been able to make a loud enough noise about sexual abuse to awaken the sleeping giant called society. When the giant fully awakens, the veil of secrecy will be removed and children will know that they have the right to say 'No' to unwanted touch (even if it *is* dear old dad). Aggressors will know that children will be more likely not only to say 'No' but also to tell someone. Children will be supported by a society ready to take responsible and knowledgeable action on their behalf.

Change has been slow, but at least it has finally begun. It has only been within the last few years that the subject of sexual abuse has been discussed on television and in newspapers and magazines. In fact, it was not until 1986 that British Telecom finally allowed the helping agencies to use the word 'incest' in their phone-book listings—before that it had not been considered 'suitable'.

Obviously, the United Kingdom is just cracking the ice, but it is a start. The start has been concerned with children: how to prevent sexual abuse, how to recognise it if it is currently happening, how to help if it has already happened. However, one large body of people has not had its needs recognised or administered to. These people are the many adults who suffered sexual abuse as children. They are no longer the 'poor little innocent children' whom society is beginning to embrace. Instead, they are guilt-ridden, self-sabotaging, sexually dysfunctioning, on-going victims. There is a list as long as your arm of problems these people can have, and helping agencies are confused about what kind of help to offer.

So far, only a small number of such victims have been able to regain their emotional health without professional intervention. Therein lies the reason for this book. The whys and wherefores of sexual abuse will be discussed, but the focus will be 'how to recover'. The message I learned personally, and share with my clients, is this: you will never *forget* what happened to you, but you can *stop hurting*. Parks Inner Child Therapy, which is what you will be learning about in this book, outlines the valuable skills needed to stop the hurting.

However, if victims have any of the following problems, they should use this book in collaboration with a therapist and not attempt to solve their problems alone: if they cannot bear physical touch, if they are sexually interested in children, if they have only vague memories of abuse happening, or if they feel extremely disturbed or out of control.

Note to Partners of Abuse Victims

If you are the partner of a victim of sexual abuse, reading this book may be rough going. To know that your partner has experienced some of the pain you will be reading about will stir up conflicting emotions. You may feel that you want to 'do something' to help your partner feel better, but this feeling may also be accompanied by the desire to turn away from the pain. Caring partners usually experience these two contradictory feelings. It is quite normal, so do not call yourself names over it.

The 'something' you can do will involve a rather passive role: *listening, supporting and giving space.*

Listening will be difficult, and sometimes you may have to stop and continue later. The story may be painful to hear or tell, so both of you should consider it permissible to stop when either person needs to. Most victims want to be able to talk about the abuse with their partner but need to choose their own time and also need to know that their partner will not turn away repulsed in any way.

Tears should be expected, but comments such as 'You poor thing' are not helpful. To convey your sorrow about your partner's experience, try statements such as 'I'm so sorry you had to go through that.' *Never* question why your partner did not tell someone or imply that any guilt is attached to her. If your partner is comfortable with touch, feel free to offer a safe cuddle. If you are unsure about whether your partner wants a cuddle, you can ask, 'Would a cuddle be welcome right now?', or just back off if your partner stiffens up when you attempt to hold her.

Support means that you are on your partner's side. Never try to help your partner understand the abuser or her mother with statements such as 'He must have been a sick man—you should feel sorry for him' or 'You can't blame your mother—she probably didn't know.' Your partner will have to come to terms with feelings about the abuser or about her mother on her own. To sound as though you are making excuses for the abuser or the mother will only delay the healing process and alienate you from your partner.

Giving space simply means allowing your partner time to

sort out emotions and reactions to memories with minimum pressure. Your own needs may have to take second place now and again, but the sacrifice will be well worth it. Your partner may be facing several months of disturbance—sometimes withdrawing from you; at other times needing extra comfort. When she works on anger exercises you may experience some of that anger spilling over on to you. Accommodate the erratic behaviour as best you can, *but* do not be afraid kindly to make your limits clear. It is a good opportunity for both of you to develop your skills in the area of compromise.

If the abuser is still alive and perhaps even living down the street, you may feel like telling the person what a dirty so-and-so you think he is. Some husbands want to beat up the abuser. Before rushing out the door to vent your anger, find out what your partner wants. If your partner is saying, 'No, don't do that' then you must honour her request. To do otherwise is to put your partner back into a powerless position—unable to stop from happening something that is frightening and confusing. If you are left with a raging anger, try the pillow-bashing exercise you will learn about later on in the book (Chapter 7) to let off steam. Your partner needs you to be supportive of her feelings, so knowing you are bashing a pillow instead of the abuser will help prove your support better than mere words could do. Respecting your partner's wishes also creates trust—a valuable commodity in any relationship.

Contributors

Throughout this book, you will be reading about several people who were sexually abused as children. Their information comes from work they did as a part of therapy. They have donated this homework so that others can learn from it and know they are not alone. The names of all these contributors have been changed, however. The first of these contributions is a poem written by a male victim we will call Richard.

Look for the Child

Look for the child that doesn't play
While others laugh and run.

Does it cross your mind why he stands alone
Instead of joining in the fun?

He never seems to have a friend
And is never a part of the crowd.
You will never hear him say very much
But inside he is screaming out loud.

He pleads for help with movement
And every unspoken word.
He shouts at the world through saddened eyes
But no one's ever heard.

Always silent and full of mistrust
With any friendship showing doubt.
He feels he can't talk to anyone
In case his secret should slip out.

He can't run up and tell you
What he is going through.
Because he feels the guilt is all his own
He feels there is nothing he can do.

He didn't go off in a stranger's car
Or take sweets from a dirty old man.
He was with somebody he trusted and loved
When his torment first began.

Please don't ignore this sad-eyed boy
Don't turn and walk away.
Show him some love and gain his trust,
Listen to what he has to say.

It may not be pleasant, it may even hurt.
But hear his story through.
Do what you can to help this child
Because it could so easily have been you.

1 Abuse

What is Sexual Abuse?

There are a number of definitions of sexual abuse, depending on the context in which it is approached—for example, the law, helping agencies or therapy. Whether sexual abuse involves fondling or penetration, the emotional damage to the child is the same, trust is destroyed. This book will therefore define sexual abuse from the context of therapy: sexual abuse is an adult involving a child in any activity from which the adult expects to derive sexual arousal. When that adult is related to the child, the term 'incest' will also be used for such abuse.

Some abused children do not have their bodies sexually interfered with; instead, they witness sexual behaviour of adults—such as exposure, masturbation or intercourse. This can damage the child's trust. One young woman described how, during her childhood, her father would expose himself to her whenever they were alone in the house. He only touched her on the arm, but she never knew when he would appear, naked and grinning foolishly. He would stand there for a short time, red in the face, with an erection, then leave the room as quickly as he arrived. The behaviour was never spoken about, and when he returned later he was dressed and behaved normally. The inappropriateness of his actions, both during and after the event, damaged the child's trust.

Other inappropriate behaviours are hugging a child up against an adult's erection, 'accidentally' fondling genitals or breasts time after time, and kisses that turn into French kissing. In these cases, there is no clothing removed and the adult acts perfectly normal afterwards. The child is left feeling confused and guilty—not knowing exactly what happened (depending on her age) and not knowing how to stop it.

We shall also discuss (in Chapter 11—Sexual Dysfunction)

the kind of damage done when a mother places her son as head of the house—in the role of a partner. Even without overt sexual activity, the inappropriate intimate nature of such a relationship erodes the child's trust in the adult. In Chapter 6 the effects of emotional abuse will be discussed. The exercises outlined in this book are effective for overcoming the effects of any childhood abuse, be it emotional, physical or sexual.

Most of the cases in this book will represent the typical type of sexual abuse experienced by the clients from my practice. Their experiences are very similar to those of the victims I worked with in America: experiences that generally consist of manual or oral genital stimulation (performed by either the abusers or the victim) and attempted or completed penetration.

Normal hugging and kissing will *not* be interpreted by the child as abuse. Many parents have become anxious and fearful about this, but children do not become frightened and confused by loving hugs and kisses—they *need* them.

However, children can respond negatively to 'bully hugging' —that is, hugging which consists of holding children against their will or tossing them in the air, ignoring their discomfort and fright. This behaviour is often accompanied by statements such as 'She's just acting like a baby' or 'She *really* loves it.' Many clients have expressed anger about treatment that ignored their right to say 'No.' It also undermines trust in the adult. ('Bully hugging' does not in any way refer to the hugging therapy being advocated in some quarters for use with autistic children.)

Sometimes parents have passing feelings of sexual stimulation when interacting with their children. The child may recognise these and/or feel stimulation as well. If these are isolated experiences and the parents had not planned them to happen, there should be no damage done. If, however, the parent finds such experiences happening more often, or is even setting up occasions where they are likely to happen, then it is time to seek help.

Abuse Cases

The following are three case histories. The stories were told to me by adults, but I have rewritten them as they were experienced, in the language a child would use. They are examples of the circumstances that children can be faced with. For those reading this book who do not have a background of sexual abuse, these histories can help you understand the type of things that children experience.

Linda (age thirteen)

My dad has been doing it to me since I can remember. He wanted a boy when I was born—I think he just never liked me since. On Fridays, when mum goes shopping, dad watches from the landing till she's out of sight. Then he locks the doors and I know what's coming next. First he gets the cane from its hiding place, then I really get it for whatever I did wrong during the week.

After the caning, he takes off my clothes and lies on top of me. He pokes at me between my legs with his thing, swearing at me all the time. He gets really angry-acting and red-faced when he's doing that. Then he stands over me and rubs his thing until the white stuff comes out on to me. After that I get another beating for any protesting I did when he was on top of me.

My mum never mentions the cane marks, and I don't think she would care about the other either.

My teacher at school was really nice. She used to like me. I told her what daddy did to me, 'cause I thought she could stop the beatings and the other. But she was angry and called me a liar. I had to stand in the waste basket at school that day, facing the wall with a sign on my back that said 'liar'. She sent a note home to dad and he came to the school, took me home and punished me.

Dad broke my arm when he hit me with a chair once. After the plaster was on I was sitting in the back garden, just hating him. Suddenly, I got a great idea to get back at him. He grew prize tomatoes and was just about ready to take them into a show. Well, since he always called me 'slug', I decided I would be one. So, I carefully ate little holes in the tomatoes, just like a slug would! He never knew it was me and he really cursed those slugs—I was glad to pay him back.

My gran came to visit soon after that and saw the cane marks on my backside when she went to look at some boils I

had there. She's going to take me to live with her. I won't tell
her about the other— I don't want her to be angry with me
like the teacher was.

Steven (age eleven)

It started one day when I went to see my friend, Grace. We
used to go horse-riding together. This time just Grace and
her father were home. He wanted Grace to walk to the shops
for something and said she could buy us some sweets too. I
started to go with her, but he said 'No', it would take too long
if we both went. So, Grace went on her own and I waited
with her father. She was going to be gone about twenty
minutes.

After she left, her father went upstairs. Then he called me
to come up there. I thought it was peculiar, but I wasn't
going to say 'No' to a grown-up. He was in the bathroom, the
door was open and he stood looking at me with his willy
outside of his trousers. I had never seen a grown man's willy
before and I felt ever so embarrassed and uncomfortable. I
didn't know where to look.

He sort of beckoned me over to him. I was very
confused— I didn't know what the point was. He put one
hand very firmly on my shoulder and put my hand on his
willy. He moved my hand up and down and then told me to
do it on my own. I kept letting go—I didn't understand. I
was really scared and my stomach felt funny and upset. He
was acting funny—sort of nervous and het-up. He seemed out
of control and was breathing funny. He told me roughly not to
let go of his willy again and kept his hand over mine, making
it move faster. All I could think was 'Why is this happening?
Why is he doing this?' Soon, some white, sticky stuff came
out of his willy. I felt like I was going to be sick. He finally
allowed me to let go.

He was calmer now and took me downstairs. He kept
saying I mustn't tell. I felt like I was in a daze or a bad dream.
Grace came back and I said I wanted to go home. Her father
walked me to the door and pushed some money in my hand
as I stepped out. I didn't know what to think—the coins
made me feel like I was made a part of it. If I told anyone he
would say I had taken money. They would think I wanted

money to do this and I knew it must be very bad, whatever it was. I knew I would never tell anyone anyway—how could I tell something so horrible? I threw the money away. I went home and stayed in my room all day. I saw him a couple of days later walking past my house. He said he was sorry about 'the other day' and told me to forget about it.

A couple of months later, I went to see if Grace could ride horses again. Her father answered the door. He said Grace was home and invited me inside. I stepped just into the hall and stood by the door. He went to the other room and called Grace. He returned, put his hand on my shoulder and said she wasn't there. He kept hold of my shoulder and marched me upstairs. I was frantic with fear, but I didn't know how to get away. I kept thinking, 'Oh no, I've got myself in this trouble again.' He must have known no one was going to be home for a long time.

He took me to the bedroom and told me to take off my clothes. I was so scared I was shaking. I could hardly undo the buttons. He took off his trousers. He made me lie on my stomach and he was acting crazy again. He took some vaseline and put it on his willy. He was nervous and kept fumbling the jar and dropping it. I felt so trapped and scared. Then he put his willy in my bum. At first, he was just poking at me with his willy—I was crying and squirming. When he poked it inside my bum, it hurt so much that I screamed out. He put his hand over my face. I knew nothing would ever be the same again— I remember thinking, 'This is the end of the world.'

I never told—how could I? It was more horrible than the other time. I started wetting the bed at night and once I even soiled it. My father was so angry with me. I had lots of nightmares and I couldn't shut out of my mind what happened. I couldn't concentrate at school and my marks were terrible. My parents said I was acting like a baby all the time. I could never tell them what happened. I wondered if other men did that to boys. I was always careful never to be alone with any man.

Peggy (age nine—American)
Did I ever try to tell? Yeah, I did tell my mum when I was six.

I got real scared, 'cause I heard at school what the 'F word' meant, and that was what my stepfather was doing to me! So, even though I was scared to tell my mum, I was *more* scared about such a bad thing happening to me.

I wasn't sure what to say. I waited till my stepfather left the house. The more I thought about it, the more I started to cry. Then I was crying so hard, I was hiccuping. My mum put me on her lap first (she doesn't do that much) and wanted to know what was wrong. When I finally told her that 'Daddy put his thing in my thing,' she was really mad. She put me off her lap and shook and shook me. She kept screaming, 'You're lying, aren't you? Aren't you? You filthy trouble-maker!' In the end I just agreed I was lying. Then I got a spanking for being a little liar.

I tried to tell again when I was eight. My aunt and mum went to the shops and left me with my uncle. They were visiting us for a week. (He was the first one who did stuff to me, ever since I lived with them for a while when I was two.)

We lived in a caravan with windows at the front and the sofa up against the window. Uncle Harry was sitting on the sofa with his trousers down around his feet. I had to take my panties off and lift up my dress and stand over his face. He did stuff to me with his mouth like that and rubbed his willy at the same time.

He told me to tell him as soon as I saw mum and auntie come round the corner. Instead, I got a good idea and didn't say anything! When the door opened, Uncle Harry was trying to move pretty fast. He still only had his trousers up to about his knees when he stumbled past mum and auntie coming in the door. His willy was showing and everything.

Well, they came in, and uncle finished running to the bedroom. I was still standing on the sofa (with my shoes on too!). Nobody said nothing. They just talked about the shopping. Finally, I put my pants on and read a funny book. Later, uncle came out of the bedroom and we all just sat around like always. Mum never even yelled at me for having my shoes on the sofa. Anyway, I guess my idea wasn't so good after all.

Richard, a male client, abused by his aunt, wrote about his experience in a poem:

Before I Sleep, I Cry

I don't like to sit upon your lap
And cuddle close to you.
I don't like it when you touch me
And do the things you do.
I know I shouldn't do it,
Although I don't know why.
But everytime it happens,
Before I sleep, I cry.

Don't tell me that it's my fault
Or that I'm the one to blame.
Because I am just a little boy
And I can't share your shame.
Don't smack me when I'm not naughty,
And don't watch me get undressed.
Don't let me see you without your clothes,
And when it's bedtime please let me rest.

Soon it will be time to go
And mum won't let you near me.
Then when I give a cry for help,
Someone will be there to hear me.
I'll be glad when I don't live here,
Then you'll leave me alone.
I'll be glad when I'm a big boy,
Then I can bath all on my own.

A Child's Message

The following drawing was done by Katy when she was seven years old. Recently she found some old school exercise books that had been stored away for years. She was astounded to discover several drawings she had made which all included light-bulbs that were almost exact replicas of circumcised penises.

These drawings coincide with her sexual-abuse trauma and are typical of drawings done by children who are attempting to alert adults to the fact that something is wrong but are too frightened to use words. In Katy's case, and for most children, no one noticed, or if they did they were not able to understand the message or confront the issue.

Loss of Trust

The natural father is the most common aggressor, according to
P. B. Mrazek, M. A. Lynch and A. Bentovim's 'Sexual Abuse
of Children in the United Kingdom' (*Child Abuse and Neglect*,
vol. 7, 1983). When I first discovered this, it surprised me. Since
my stepfather had been the main aggressor in my life, I had
comforted myself with the fantasy that 'My real father wouldn't
do this to me.' That fantasy was particularly important to me,
as from the age of two until almost thirteen I had been sexually
abused by five other relatives besides my stepfather. I needed
to feel that, at least, *real* fathers do not have sex with their
children. I was saddened to find out differently.

Generally children regard their genitals simply as for toilet
purposes until puberty, when they begin to realise that there
are sexual uses as well. An abuser makes the child aware of the
sexual functions her body (and his too) is capable of well before
the time at which this would normally happen—he physically
identifies her sexuality prematurely. However, any trusted
adult—especially a father or father figure—who introduces sex
into his relationship with a child does much more than
prematurely make the child physically aware of her sexuality.
He removes not only innocence but also trust, which is an
essential building block for a child's emotional development.
No longer an innocent child, she has adult information that
must be kept secret at all costs. Because she lives in fear that
someone will discover the secret, she often avoids making close
relationships, believing that discovery will lead to her becoming
a social outcast. As one boy stated, 'I knew what was done to
murderers, and murder was talked about. What was happening
to me wasn't even talked about, so I couldn't imagine what the
consequences might be.'

Self-sabotage

When trust in parental figures is lost, an essential link with the
adult world is severed. Child victims are emotionally on their
own, with guilt, fear and feelings of inadequacy as companions.
Many remain fixed at that child level of emotional development,
as though the trauma put a stop on time. Adult information

and knowledge are added as they grow up, but the underlying guilt, fear and inadequacy remain and govern much of their decision-making.

The governing power of these feelings is seen in the compulsion to sabotage such happiness as comes their way. Relationships are strained to breaking-point by constant demands for proof of love (which can never be believed), by chronic jealousy (which cannot be comforted), by endless emotional tests (programmed for failure) and by sexual dysfunction (since pleasure is not allowed to the guilty).

Job success can be sabotaged, as well as health, friendships and even general social interaction. The burden of guilt demands punishment. Any set-backs or problems that occur in life can become verification of inadequacy—victims have the feeling that 'There is something terribly wrong with me or the sexual abuse wouldn't have happened, and this problem proves it.' Sometimes this idea of intrinsic inadequacy is reinforced from the start by the aggressor—'I wouldn't do this if you were a good girl'—or the child simply assumes that she is now bad because a bad thing has happened to her. Childhood friendships that drift apart can be perceived by the abused child as proof that she is 'defective'. As she grows up, normal losses in life—jobs, friendships, romance (not to mention serious losses such as death, health, etc.)—are simply regarded as further proof of guilt and inadequacy. Of course, proof of guilt requires more punishment, so the vicious circle continues.

When crisis becomes part of an abused child's life, it is then regarded as a normal situation. In the words of one counsellor from a refuge for battered women:

I have observed countless episodes of women who throw their lives into crisis when things become too peaceful. They seem to connect a sense of security with living in a continual crisis situation. As, because of childhood abuse, they have also come to connect love with pain, they need to be taught about self-sabotaging behaviour. Discussion of what a 'normal' relationship entails is also imperative.

The need for crises often extends to relationships with friends, family and children. I have also discussed with clients the fact that advertising and the media reinforce these 'love = pain' delusions. Commercials and soap operas seem to be the worst offenders and have an undue amount of influence on a woman who suffers from low self-esteem.

2   Abusers

The abuser does not see the damage done by his sexual activity—he is busy weaving an intricate web of justification to relieve himself of responsibility for the sexual and emotional crime he is committing against a trusting child. In some cases, the aggressor looks upon the relationship as 'special'. Someone else's incestuous relationship may seem sordid and horrible, but his own is 'different'. Justifications akin to this, that may be more familiar, are often found in the attitudes of adults in adulterous relationships: 'He's got himself a bit on the side. But, of course, with *us* it's different—it's real love.'

The reasons aggressors give for sexually abusing their children are almost laughable: 'I wanted to teach her what to expect from boys' or 'I was teaching her right from wrong' or 'I was punishing her for being bad.' One aggressor explained, 'It was different with my daughter and me. She *wanted* me to make love to her.' How did he know? 'She got on the bed when I was in my underpants and kissed me.' How old was she? 'Seven.'

It is an inadequate male's fantasy that a child seduces him. 'You made me do it' may originally be told to a child as a form of emotional blackmail, but too often the abuser begins to believe it himself. One father of four daughters—all sexually abused by him—was shocked and angry to be arrested for the crime. As policemen led him away, he was heard to complain about their interference in his private affairs. (In other words, he so firmly believed that his daughters all wanted him sexually that he considered them to be his own harem. He brought them up, and he believed that this gave him the right to have sex with them.)

The reasons given by abusers have little to do with reality. They rarely see what they did as causing serious harm. Many are convinced that the child liked it. Forgetting his threats, bribes and intimidation, the aggressor sometimes views the broken will of the child as an agreement to the act: 'She never tried to hit me or shout at me, so I thought she liked it.'

What Kind of Men Abuse?

People often shake their heads in disbelief and wonder what kind of men sexually abuse children. When discussing the strangers who commit 14% of such crimes, we are generally discussing paedophiles—adults whose sexual preference is children. Gay Search's *The Last Taboo* (Penguin, 1988) quotes Ray Wyre, a counsellor working with sexual abusers of children in England, as reporting 50 to 1000 as the number of children one paedophile may interfere with during his lifetime.

Frequently paedophiles look for a child who needs 'time' with adults. Some parents rarely sit down and talk to their children or spend time in an activity geared to the child's age. Some even spend as little time with their children as possible. These children are easy game for any adult intent on sexual abuse. Such adults usually come from the other group of aggressors: the 86% who are within the family. Paedophiles are not confined to the role of 'stranger'—according to Gay Search's book mentioned above, many look for single-parent families and form a relationship with the mother to gain access to the children. Often these men look like a 'good catch'— kind, gentle and very keen on children.

Family aggressors are not generally paedophiles, however— they are usually active, heterosexual men, but their sexual abuse of children is not specifically a sexually motivated act. It has more to do with power and aggression.

Most abusers are men with little control or power over their own life. Feeling inadequate and powerless with their peers, they turn towards children to express control and power. They may do so by means of physical, sexual or emotional abuse.

The following example may be of help in understanding how the abuser is motivated by power and aggression rather than sexual desire. If at some point the child feels pleasure from genital stimulation and consequently responds by making an overt advance towards the abuser, the child may find the abuser suddenly angry. The child may be harshly rebuked and the abuser withdraw from further sexual interaction. Clients usually admit a lot of shame and guilt about scenes like that and also feel very confused—'That's what he wanted, wasn't it?' The answer is, 'No.' The abuser was sexually stimulated by the fact that he was in charge of the sexual interaction. When the child responded independently, the abuser was no longer in total control. Vulnerability and fear in the child were the turn-on. Without those, the abuser became impotent.

ABUSER PROFILE

Incest is relentlessly democratic, with victims being white or black, male or female, any age in childhood, fat or skinny, ugly or beautiful, poor or wealthy or middle-class. However, the profile of the abuser is more easily established.

Most abusers are emotionally immature. They either have a low level of control over their behaviour or are rigidly over-controlled. They have low self-esteem. Many have an authoritarian background. Many were abused themselves as children.

In *Conspiracy of Silence—the Trauma of Incest* (Volcano Press (US), 1985) Sandra Butler tells us:

Men who are reported as incestuous aggressors seldom have prior criminal records. They have little or no psychiatric history, are not necessarily excessive drinkers and appear to be of average intelligence and education. Their work histories are steady, and their marital histories primarily monogamous. Like most of the male population they have few or no ways to identify, understand or ventilate their feelings in an ultimately coherent or cathartic manner. Like most men, too, they have had few, if any, examples of loving and tender males in their lives and therefore come to emulate faithfully the only model they do have. That model is one we all know well: the man who is strong, sexually virile and competitive with other men in the outside world, and who is powerful in his own home, boss with his wife and authoritarian with his children. However, it is the case with many aggressors that when this socially prescribed model of behaviour becomes inaccessible to them, with all other definitions of maleness rendered unacceptable by our culture, they turned to what they had been conditioned to believe is the final source of their strength: their genitals, which become their weapon, their catharsis, and their downfall.

An abusing father may use his child as a stand-in wife. Charming and respected outside the home, he takes a weak wife who is seen as cold and bitter, thereby justifying his own self-pity and earning him the sympathy of others, who may include his daughter. The role of wife and mother may be slowly shifted to the child. Being of help to 'poor daddy' at first gives her a feeling of importance, but soon the child is overwhelmed by the burden of this role. She has been subtly trapped by her father. The girl's life may now be caring for younger brothers or sisters or other domestic work and servicing dad's sexual needs. The father's role in setting up this situation and the mother's passive, withdrawn attitude are overlooked by the child. Instead she blames herself for taking her mother's place, thinking that that is even the reason daddy had sex with her. This childhood perception stays on un-challenged, battering her with guilt into adult life.

For the abuser there was a confusion of roles. The child was regarded as something other than a child—perhaps as a surrogate for someone else. Perhaps he was attempting to relate to the child in a way in which he could not relate to his wife. The damage done to the child might never even have been considered.

Another abuser is the misogynous father. ('Misogyny' means 'hatred of women'.) A high percentage of such offenders come from authoritarian backgrounds and/or professions with rigid or extreme controls, such as police work, the clergy and the armed forces. The misogynous father is more likely also to employ verbal and physical abuse, using family members to act out power games. Children do not normally question obedience to an authoritarian father and have no illusions of mother being able to support or help them. Offenders in this category may be highly respected within the community, which isolates the child even more—few children feel that they will be believed if their abuser is a policeman, the vicar or a pillar of the community.

Female Abusers

There are fewer examples of female abusers (but see Chapter 11), but what is known shows that they use the same blackmail techniques as their male counterparts. The myth that they would be more loving and kind, helping a young boy reach manhood, should be shattered by this next example.

The following passage is from Richard's 'inner child', explaining how his aunt had introduced him to intercourse when he was aged eleven. (He had experienced three years of other forms of sexual abuse by her so far, and had two more years ahead.)

Richard

After the time in the bathroom, I was told to get dressed and go and sit on my bed to wait for her. When she came in she was holding a book and a newspaper. She sat next to me and asked me if I had enjoyed what had happened. I said, 'Yes' because if you say 'No' to her then you are punished. She said did I know what I had just done. I said, 'Had sex.' She said, 'Yes, but do you know what incest means?' She passed me the book and told me to look it up. I couldn't spell it so she told me, but I still couldn't find it. She snatched the book back and found it and told me to read what it meant. I read some of it but I couldn't read it all so Aunt Ellen read it out for me. I still didn't understand so she said it meant having sex with a relative could send you to jail.

She then asked if I knew what rape was. Without waiting for an answer, she looked it up and read it out. It sounded like what I had done with her. She then opened the newspaper and showed me a story about a man who had been jailed for ten years for rape. I thought I was going to jail and started to cry. Aunt Ellen put her arms around me and told me not to worry as she would never tell anyone. But she said I had to promise that every time my willy got hard I had to tell her by saying, 'I need to rape you again, Auntie.' She said that way I wouldn't rape anyone else and go to prison. Every time I got hard I was so scared I told her and we would have sex.

Alcohol

Alcoholism can add more heartache to an already dismal situation, and for some men it acts as a catalyst to commit the act. It is not the reason for the incest happening in the first place. Using alcohol does not make an aggressor want to molest children, but it can be useful in blurring his sense of responsibility while he molests.

3 Mother

'I hate my mother as much as I hate my stepfather for what he did to me. He started on me when I was four. I told her when I was six, and she called me a liar. She wouldn't save me—she let it happen! I hate her!'

No, this is not an isolated case: some mothers told by their children of an incestuous situation choose to disbelieve them. Only a few mothers take any action against the aggressor if he is a relative—even fewer if he is their husband.

Mothers Who Know

The mother who chooses to disbelieve her child is no different from the society she lives in. It is much easier to call the child a liar than to break the family apart, running a grave risk of financial ruin, social scorn and feelings of guilt and failure. Frequently, the aggressor vehemently denies the accusation of sexual abuse, so that makes it much easier to label the child as a trouble-maker and punish her for saying such a terrible thing about her father.

In most incestuous families, there is not a trusting atmosphere to encourage communication. (In fact, it is rare indeed to find incest within a family which teaches and practises communication and respect.) The mother may be equally as emotionally inadequate as her offending partner, shutting out painful information and putting a wall up around the subject—sometimes for the rest of her life.

Examining the cases of sexual abuse of clients from my practice, as many as two-thirds of mothers knew of the sexual abuse. (Only a small number actually jointly participated in the abuse.) The mothers became silent, colluding partners—on some level knowing of their child's plight, but not stepping in to stop it. Some were told by their children and denied the abuse, while others ignored clues and never questioned suspect behaviour. It became a case of 'We don't see what we see, hear what we hear or know what we know' for *all* members of the family.

A colluding mother may not question her husband if he leaves the bedroom during the night for over an hour or if he insists on sleeping for part of the night in the child's room when there is no immediate reason to, such as the child having bad dreams or fearing the dark. She may not question the child's reluctance to be alone with the father or any sudden negative behaviour demonstrated by the child. The father of one of my clients locked himself in the bedroom with his daughter and simply told the mother to stay out. She did, without question, ignoring the child's screams. In my own life, my stepfather would spend many nights in my bed, or even subtly molest me in the same bed with my mother.

It is always difficult to come to terms with the fact that your marriage or relationship is in serious trouble. How much more devastating it must be to know that your partner is a child-molester. Anyone would say, 'This can't be true.' The mother, using denial as her only coping skill, says, 'This *isn't* true.' Since society as a whole has not wanted to face the ugliness of incest, it is not surprising that an emotionally inadequate and dependent mother wants to turn away too. Unfortunately, that leaves the child to face it—alone.

UNWANTED FAMILY INTERVENTION
Sometimes other members of the family (aunts, older brothers or sisters, etc.) will suspect that abuse is happening and put pressure on the mother to investigate. If the mother already knows (or has strong suspicions) but does not want to face the issue, she will sabotage the enquiry.

Victims have reported being angrily summoned before mother and sometimes another relative as well. With the atmosphere heavy with hostility, the child would then have been asked if something was 'going on', or perhaps 'Has anyone touched your private parts?' Because the mother's behaviour was angry and threatening, the child's resulting answer was predictable—denial.

Most victims with this experience were sure that their mother did not want to know the truth and that she was approaching the subject only because others had pressured her to do so. They report having felt that the underlying message was 'Don't you dare tell.' They didn't, and consequently sealed off any avenue for doing so in future. Most feel a strong sense of guilt when they look back on the experience, accusing and blaming themselves for not telling when the opportunity was there.

A common mistake that victims make is to judge themselves as children by the information they now have as adults. But children *do not have* the sophistication or knowledge to assess their own or others' behaviour. Children merely react to the strongest influence around them. When things go wrong, children usually blame themselves. It is easier for children to blame themselves than to face the reality that their father (or a trusted adult) betrayed them and their mother could not (or would not) save them. By blaming themselves, that painful information is kept hidden. They trade that unbearable truth for a lifetime of self-sabotage. But that truth *can* be faced and survived.

Mothers Who Did Not Know

Some mothers did not know on any level what was happening in their home. Once the incest was found out, they supported the child and either ended the relationship with the aggressor or sought family therapy. Those mothers may or may not have reported it to the authorities, depending on their circumstances.

Mothers who did not know about the abuse nevertheless suffer from guilt and self-recrimination over the many clues they can see in retrospect. These will have been clues that parents could have easily overlooked, and may take various forms, including sleeplessness, returning to babyish behaviour, school difficulties, unusual behaviour shifts, new fears, clinging, bed-wetting, sexual knowledge beyond the child's years, and needing more reassurance. A few of these behaviours are present in any child; however, the abused child will show almost all of them.

AFTER MOTHER KNOWS

A mother who discovers that her child has been abused must

try not to become bogged down in her own guilt over what has already happened. Instead, it is now time to give her child reassurance and support. Belief, not blame, and assurance that love has not changed are the greatest gifts a mother can give her victimised child.

Those same gifts are just as essential to the adult woman who finally reveals a childhood sexual abuse to her mother. Her adult needs are the same as when she was a child. She wants to hear her mother say how sorry she is that it happened and that she was not able to save her. She needs acknowledgement of the emotional pain she has suffered. She wants to know that her mother condemns the aggressor and does not blame her. And, finally, she wants to be comforted.

People may assume that all mothers will meet these needs instinctively. Unfortunately, the victim of sexual abuse is often met with a denial of responsibility rather than an apology. She finds her emotional pain dismissed with 'You seem to have recovered OK' or 'You never seemed upset' or perhaps even 'You always made a big fuss over anything—how was I supposed to know that *that* was happening.' The mother often excuses the aggressor—'He must have been a sick man; you should have compassion on him' or 'It's not right to hate your own father'—then accuses the victim: 'What did you do to lead him on?' or 'Why would he do that when he could have turned to me?' The adult or child victim needs to be held and comforted, but the guilt-ridden mother will usually turn away, withdrawing physically and remaining cold and distant. This rejection leaves strong resentment and bitterness for the victim to add to her already heavy emotional baggage.

Some mothers are never confronted with the truth of their child's experience, because they appear too emotionally weak to bear the confrontation. The child shoulders the responsibility and even into adult life is reluctant to tell mother, because 'It would ruin her.' The victim may spend a lifetime protecting her mother, and despising her for being so weak. The repressed anger and guilt can take a very high toll, for there is no one left for the victim to confront but herself. She whips herself with phobias, fears and self-sabotage with all the venom she can never show her mother.

Mothers' Backgrounds

Mothers of incest victims are often found to be vulnerable people themselves. Some were even sexually abused as children. It seems that few came from loving, supporting homes. There were no role-models displaying nurturing attitudes to these mothers, and they do not know how to present themselves as positive role-models to their own children. Inadequately prepared to cope with life, they follow the pattern they are used to.

A mother whose background was lacking in love, support and nurturing, and who may also have been sexually abused herself, is likely to choose an emotionally inadequate partner. (See *Women Who Love Too Much*—details are given in the Book List at the end of this book.) The stage is then set for incest to develop. This family may be rich or poor, intelligent or under-achieving. Its members may come from any walk of life, but they share the same emotional inadequacies. When incest happens, the mother is faced with an enormous problem. She faces fears that would shake the strongest person—fear of facing the problem alone, fear of financial disaster, fear of retaliation by her husband, fear of the social stigma, fear of becoming entangled with the law—and lack of faith in helping agencies. Some may be able to reach out for help with these overwhelming problems, but many others do not know how to begin. They cannot step in to save their children because they cannot even save themselves.

Aggressors and society often lay the blame on mothers: 'It wouldn't have happened if she had not been frigid [working, ill, unbalanced, etc.]' However, there are many women who are working, ill, unbalanced or frigid whose husbands do *not* have sex with their children. Although mothers have their own problems to sort out and answer for, the fact is that abuse would not have happened if the aggressor had not chosen to commit it. The blame for sexual abuse lies nowhere except with the aggressor.

4 Guilt

Guilt is the most difficult hurdle for the victim of child abuse to jump. Once guilt is resolved, much of the self-sabotaging behaviour stops. There will be small bouts now and again as forgotten memories surface, but, once the initial battle is over, other episodes are more easily handled. Understanding and conquering guilt is the key to regaining emotional health, so ways to do so will be pointed out in most chapters in this book as they apply to each subject.

Keep in mind, however, that some victims are able to realise that they have nothing to feel guilty about. These people are usually facing their biggest battles with crippling feelings of betrayal, experienced as an emotionally paralysing sadness.

Parents Omnipotent

As small children, we see our parents as gods—able to do anything and all-knowing. We depend on them for everything. Unfortunately, parenthood deifies no one, and some pitifully inadequate parents are more demonic than god-like.

Even if children begin to see their parents behave violently, irrationally or sexually towards them, they feel a need to excuse that confusing and frightening behaviour. Somehow it cannot be that these god-like parents are defective: it is easier to take the blame themselves than to threaten the basic security of parental superiority. Children are usually listening to blaming statements anyway—'Look what you made me do now' or 'I wouldn't have lost my temper if you hadn't . . .' Feeling that parents know everything, children believe that somehow they are to blame for their parents' poor behaviour. When sexual abuse starts, this pattern of blame and guilt continues.

Pleasurable Feelings

If there were any pleasurable sensations during fondling or sexual activity, guilt increases. For many children, actual intercourse is never accomplished or even tried. The aggressor could be fearful of damaging the child and being found out (especially if it is a small child), or perhaps the aggressor finds intercourse too threatening and limits his sexual behaviour to manual and oral activities. In any case, the sexual abuse is often done gently, without overt violence. (That in itself causes confusion—children are used to 'bad' people being angry and rough and 'nice' people being gentle and smiling.)

Our genitals were designed to be responsive to touch, especially gentle touch—it is not 'bad' to feel good when our genitals are touched. So, the act itself is not 'bad': what is 'bad' is the fact that an adult is doing the act to a child. So, having pleasant feelings does not mean that the child is bad; it only means that her genitals are working properly.

Consider a similar example. If a six-year-old child were shown how to operate a car by a trusted adult and, in the process of driving the car, killed someone, what or who would be to blame? Certainly not the act of driving. Certainly not the child, too young to understand the responsibility and danger. The blame would fall on the shoulders of the adult, for introducing an adult activity to a child. Should this child never drive again when she grows up? Should this child never enjoy driving when she grows up? Should this child feel guilty over the accident for the rest of her life? Should the child feel guilty because the act of driving was nice and made her feel important? The child, of course, should drive as an adult, and enjoy driving, without guilt. If the child felt important while engaging in an adult activity, that is normal. Obviously, all the same points are true for victims of sexual abuse.

'Badness'

One emotional blackmail line an abuser employs to justify himself and ensure the child's secrecy is 'You made me do it' or 'You wanted me to do it.' The child then grows up believing there is some horrible 'badness' inside her, so horrible that it could 'make a good person like daddy do bad things'. This childhood belief is seldom challenged during adult life, because by then it is an integral part of the person's identity. Needless to say, this person's guilt is deep and difficult to reach, for to face the guilt would be to face the 'badness'. A whole lifetime can be spent in running from the 'badness' or in acting it out to ensure punishment. The father who started this vicious circle of guilt often continues with the punishment by being unsupportive and critical of his now adult child.

Who's to Blame?

When giving talks to groups of professionals or lay persons on childhood sexual abuse. I am sometimes asked if a father can be blamed if his well-developed fourteen-year-old daughter seduces him. The questioners usually describe a scene where the daughter is wearing a nightie and presses herself to her father, giving him a French kiss. They ask, 'Can the father be blamed if he succumbs to such a temptation?'

First, I explain that only a small percentage of sexual abuse starts during puberty. Puberty is often when full intercourse begins for a child who has been used sexually from an average age of eight. The scene that has been described is unlikely to occur, except in the mind of someone who wants to abuse or someone who cannot accept the fact that fathers abuse. However, let us look realistically at the scene and see it clearly.

For a fourteen-year-old girl to be fully developed physically is no reason for her to be sexually abused, or every father would be an abuser. Nor should it be unusual for the same girl to wear a nightie in the presence of her father. To expect children to be embarrassed about their bodies in front of their parents (or at all) is unrealistic and emotionally unhealthy. During adolescence, most young people feel uncomfortable for a time while they adjust to the changes their bodies are experiencing. Girls especially tend to cover up rather than expose themselves during this time. It is for parents to be supportive and understanding—not pressuring their children—just giving space and time for adjustment.

During puberty, young people are often very unsure of themselves sexually. It is a time when first sexual encounters are difficult to attempt—fears of rejection and not knowing how to do things properly tend to overwhelm courage. (Many of us can remember practising kissing on the mirror or perhaps the bend of the elbow.) If it is frightening to approach peers, how much more frightening must it be to make an overt first move to an adult? But, for the sake of argument, let us say that this young girl in our scene does approach her father and French kisses him while pressing herself against him. Does he have no choice but to sexually abuse her? Is her behaviour a signal that she now wants to introduce sex into their relationship?

No—the adult always has a choice. Children are tied to the whims of their parents, not vice versa. The father in our scene should gently remove his daughter's arms from around him and, holding her hands in a caring manner, explain 'Love, I always enjoy a kiss and a cuddle with you, but the way you were kissing me just now should be saved for a boyfriend. It's a bit inappropriate between dads and daughters, so you save it for some young man you think is special.' In that way, the inappropriate behaviour is gently explained and the daughter's budding sexuality is not rejected or exploited.

It is the parents who should set limits for children in all matters. It is the parents who have years of experience to draw upon for decision-making, not the child. It is the parents' role to set limits in a firm and understanding manner, without ridicule or using the child's naïvety to the parents' advantage. If parents find themselves with repeated temptations, be they for sexual, physical or emotional abuse, it is their responsibility to get professional help before there is any danger of succumbing to temptation. The responsibility for acts of abuse against children, whatever the nature, falls on the shoulders of the adult, never the child.

Finally, no—the girl in our scene is not saying by her actions that she now wants to bring sex into her relationship with her father. Normally, a young girl should learn sexuality by observing her mother and try out flirting on her father. Safe limits are set, and the child's sexuality develops in a healthy manner. Unfortunately, many parents have trouble understanding their own sexuality and are ill-prepared to assist their children through puberty in a kind and understanding way.

5   Self-sabotage

As stated in Chapter 4, the problems sexual-abuse victims suffer stem from feelings of misplaced guilt, and these problems manifest themselves as self-sabotage. The problems of different victims are similar, but vary in as much that each personality devises an 'individual punishment programme'. The one consistent feature is that feelings of guilt require punishment. Many victims, therefore, become emotionally bankrupt, paying a debt that actually belongs to the aggressor. The aggressor should be the one suffering problems that stem from guilt, since guilt about the abuse really belongs to him. Instead, the aggressor projects blame and guilt on to the child and the child accepts that projection as truth. It is like life imprisonment for a crime that someone else has committed.

'Something Terrible'

Most victims report feeling as though they are running from an unspoken fear—a fear that they are a monstrous person. They do not know exactly why they are so monstrous, because they have never had the courage to stop, turn around and say, 'OK, what about me is so horrible?' It is a fear that developed in childhood, so it is full of misinformation and childish perceptions. It is a feeling that 'something' about them made the sexual abuse happen. This idea is reinforced by statements by abusers: 'You made me do it' or 'You wanted it.' It is also reinforced if there were multiple aggressors.

Sexual abuse by multiple aggressors is not so uncommon, and there is a simple explanation for it. The aggressors have simply recognised a vulnerable child. Just as a paedophile targets a vulnerable child, so does the family aggressor. It is easy enough to recognise a child who does not have much, if any, parental support; a child who is not listened to; a child whom the parents avoid contact with.

Once a vulnerable child is available, the family aggressor can move in easily. He can be a friendly uncle who 'loves kids' and wants to take them somewhere all the time, or a friendly neighbour who offers to babysit frequently because he just 'loves kids'. Any adult who wants to spend a *lot* of time with kids may be suspect. Children can be quite boring—their conversation repetitive and self-centred. So what does this adult gain from the relationship? If the child becomes reluctant to go with the adult, ask why and listen to the answer! Too often, the child is told 'Go with Uncle Charlie. You don't want to hurt his feelings do you?' The protests are lost—fear, guilt and a lack of knowledge keep the child trapped.

In my own life, I was sure there was something terribly wrong with me to make all those nice relatives want to sexually abuse me. As I grew up, I tried to put this 'something terrible' behind me. Once I stopped the abuse, I wanted to pretend I was normal like everyone else. I certainly did not want to talk or think about it—I might make something go wrong again—so I adopted the ostrich method of coping. Unfortunately, ignoring a problem does not make it go away. Since my childhood perception of the sexual abuse was that I was the one who somehow made it all happen, I was inwardly determined to be punished. It still never occurred to me to really examine what the 'something terrible' could be, as it was too frightening to face.

Sabotaging Relationships

'DO YOU LOVE ME?'
As a young adult, I wanted desperately to be loved and cared for. I wanted to feel special and important to someone. I wanted to be called all the pet names I was never called as a child. I could not see it then, but I was wanting a partner to come along and parent me as I should have been parented as a child. At the same time, I felt very undeserving of all that I wanted, because of the 'something terrible'.

I married at eighteen to a man of twenty-three. One of the big attractions for me was his easy-going temperament—he laughed a lot and hardly ever got angry. (In my family, people were often angry, and it seemed that laughter was rarely heard.) But even his easy-going nature became frazzled by my continual need for reassurance. One day in frustration he said, 'Will you please quit asking me every half an hour if I love you?' I was shocked: how could he say such an unkind thing to me? I quickly found out he was slightly wrong—to my horror, I discovered I was biting back the question about every *twenty* minutes! No wonder he was exasperated with me. My problem was simple: I could not believe I was lovable. At the same time, I wanted to be loved, so I kept asking. Yet, nothing he could have said or done would have convinced me that he did love me.

JEALOUSY

Chronic jealousy over any time my husband spent away from me was a very destructive force in our marriage. I am sure it looked to him as though I wanted him with me continuously (except for work), repeating every fifteen minutes like a parrot 'I love you, I love you.' To be quite honest, that was pretty close to the truth.

EMOTIONAL TESTS

I would set emotional tests that a person would have to be a mind-reader to pass, sitting back smugly saying to myself, 'See, that proves you don't love me' when he inevitably failed. I expected him to understand all my innermost thoughts and needs without ever having shared them with him. I was setting him up as the omnipotent parent who would *have* to fail to love me, because I knew that the 'something terrible' in me made me unlovable. I could not let anything good happen to me, because I did not believe I deserved it. Sometimes those thoughts would be distinct, but mostly I was acting on an inner prodding I did not question and certainly did not understand.

SEXUAL TESTS

Sexual dysfunction was not as great a problem to me as it is to many people who are sexual-abuse victims. I was not afraid of sex, nor repulsed by it. However, I used sex as another means for proof of love, which can be a big turn-off to one's partner, as it was to mine. Of course, the more he backed away, the more I demanded, and then felt unloved and rejected.

The above are just a few ways in which victims can sabotage a relationship—ways to punish themselves for a crime they think they have committed. After all, why should someone as bad, dirty or terrible as they think they are be happy? At the same time, they seldom see themselves as really setting up these circumstances. They seem to be happening spontaneously, and are viewed as verifying their feelings of being 'bad, dirty or terrible'.

Sabotaging Success

Sometimes a victim may sabotage a job that is going well, or perhaps a promotion coming up. She might be a student with ability and a good academic record, but with finals coming up she becomes ill, irritable, anxious, suffers from severe mental block, etc. so that her final results are lower than they should be. Victims are not necessarily aware at the time that they have any responsibility for what befalls them.

Sabotaging Health

Some victims use illnesses or phobias to punish themselves. As they are frequently ill or fearful, they cannot enjoy life to its fullest—sometimes to the point that they become practically, or completely, housebound. Self-mutilation is another punishment victims can display. They may disfigure their bodies by cutting themselves. They may claw their skin raw, bite themselves or bang their head repeatedly against a wall. The anger that a victim has never expressed to her abuser or mother comes out at full force at the only person she knows how to punish—herself.

Partners as a Punishment

Many victims choose a partner who has punishing behaviour of some type. They feel it is all they deserve. Sometimes they never question staying with the partner, or they may keep a fantasy of a loving relationship in their mind but never actually go out and look for one. If they change partners, often it is for another punishing type. After all, that is what feels 'normal' to them. (An excellent book describing this experience is Robin Norwood's *Women Who Love Too Much*—refer to the Book List at the back of this book for details.)

Other victims may choose a partner who is very much a father image—someone older, established and mostly domineering. (This can be someone like the victim's own father or someone who is fatherly in the more normal sense.) The 'child' within them is still looking for a supportive, loving parent. Maybe a victim will find a partner who is for some reason—perhaps through race, religion or class—not acceptable to her parents. This is a way of indirectly punishing her parents. One of my white clients had married a black man and came to me quite distressed. 'I can see I originally married my husband to get back at my parents. What should I do now?' Her ten-year relationship with her husband was very solid and positive, so I suggested that, if her marriage was a happy one, then it did not matter how it got started—she should just enjoy it. If she had chosen her partner for negative reasons and was miserably unhappy, she might think about a change, but in her case what started out for 'sabotage' reasons had turned out well.

Some female victims marry abusers. (Many of those husbands may also have been victims themselves.) When abuse of their own children starts, it is almost impossible for these women to face. It brings back all the pain and guilt they have never come to terms with. They may project all those aroused feelings of guilt, pain and anger on to the child, accusing the child of 'asking for it' as they are secretly afraid they themselves did as a child. Their life seems to be spiralling downwards. Skilled family counselling by professionals trained in this specific area can be particularly helpful at this time.

However, not every victim chooses a damaged partner—some find a loving, supportive person who can be instrumental in assisting them back to emotional health.

6 Parenting Exercises

As I explained in Chapter 1, when trust in parental figures is lost, a vital link with the adult world is severed. The child now has only guilt, fear and inadequacy as companions. Many children then stay locked in their present level of emotional maturity, as though the trauma put a stop on time. Adult information and knowledge are added, but the underlying guilt, fear and inadequacy govern their behaviour. So let us take another look at this 'stop on time'.

Inside every adult who was sexually abused are the feelings of the little child she once was. That little girl is still frightened, confused and crying—waiting to be comforted by parents who will never come for her. (Victims may already have a mental image of themselves a child forming as they read this.) That child needs to be reached, needs to be comforted, needs information about what has happened to her.

The need to be held lovingly, to have her hair stroked, to be gently rocked and soothed, is as important today as it was then. Until the 'child' is comforted, the 'adult' may not be able to take the governing role in her life. There follow a few exercises to help comfort the 'child' and allow it to begin to feel secure, so that victims can face life as a whole adult, in charge of themselves. Information must be communicated about the abuse to the 'child' until both 'child' and 'adult' fully believe it. The 'child' needs to understand why the abuse happened to her, that she is not 'bad' and that she deserves to love and be loved.

Writing

This first exercise is a writing exercise to comfort and soothe the distressed child within. In a quiet place, the 'adult' side of the victim allows the image of herself as a child to become as clear as possible. She begins a letter to the 'child', giving love, information and support—saying all the things the 'child' wanted and needed to hear so much all those years ago. The adult can use pet names for the 'child' if she likes. Tears can usually be expected—if they become too strong, she can stop and cry until they pass. The writing should be similar to the examples featured in this chapter.

The overall background of abuse should be explained, as now seen through adult eyes. Information, support and love should be given. Information that the child's feelings and reactions were normal and any child would have felt the same. Information that the adults were wrong to do what they did and that the child was not in any way responsible, for children do not have the power or knowledge to stop adults. Information of what healthy parenting is—in other words, what should have happened instead of what did. Support simply means telling the 'child' that she will never experience those things again and that you (the adult) will help her understand and overcome the things that happened to her. Love is given by just saying 'I love you.'

Making themselves familiar with the overall subject of sexual abuse of children helps victims know how to explain to their inner child what happened. (Susan Forward and Craig Buck's *Betrayal of Innocence* and Gay Search's *The Last Taboo* are two good books that contain insightful information on the subject of child sexual abuse—refer to the Book List at the end of the book for details.) The 'child' should not be viewed as bad or 'a brat' or in any other negative way. Some clients have such a negative opinion of themselves as a child that they do not want to make contact. They reject their 'child' just as their parents did. That mistake must not be made. Their 'child' needs their love and approval, and they, as the adult, need to give it. They need to make contact with the 'child' so that the emotional link with the adult world is re-established and the 'child' can learn to feel secure at last.

LOGIC VERSUS FEELINGS

Understanding with adult logic does not change feelings. Many victims are confused because they know all the logical reasons why they are not to blame, but they nevertheless cannot turn off the guilty feelings. These feelings come from the 'child'. Communicating, by writing, *secures* the information and then changes the 'child' feelings or beliefs. The information must be repeated until it shows in behaviour change. *Repeating this information through the letters is how the 'child' becomes healthy and, consequently, the adult can stop being affected by guilt, shame, anger, etc.*

It is important to address the 'child' with an adult's voice, *not* with a parent's. Although the information given will be similar to that of a parent—and essentially 'parenting' is being done—the adult should not refer to herself as 'mummy'. It is important to keep a separate identity from that of a parent.

Here is a letter written by a male victim to his 'child'.

Richard

Dear Richard

I would like to speak to you about the things that happened while you stayed at Aunt Ellen's.

I know it must be very hard for you to understand how a grown-up, who was there to look after you, could hurt and misuse someone who placed all his trust in her. You were not wrong to trust her, and you were not wrong to do the things you did. It is Aunt Ellen who was wrong—she knew that you needed love, as every child does, but she used your need for love to meet her own needs and to feed her sickness.

Don't hate your body because it reacted to her—that is the way nature intended your body to be, and anyone placed in the same position would have had the same reaction. Don't feel guilty because you did not tell anyone—that sickness makes people like Aunt Ellen very cunning. She knew Uncle Geoff had just gone to prison and the threat of you going to prison, if anyone found out, was bound to keep you quiet.

I am sorry for the things that have happened, but I promise that it is over now and I vow that nobody will ever hurt you again. Don't carry any of the guilt for Aunt Ellen—the guilt is all hers, and she must carry it on her own.

Here is a letter from a female victim to her 'child'.

Katy

Dear Child

Many years ago you were in a very unhappy situation. The people who should have been protecting and supporting you let you down. Your stepfather abused you, your mother ignored you, and the rest of the family just didn't care at all. But none of this was your fault. You were too little to be able to defend yourself or to understand what was happening. Those people shouldn't have been in charge of you, because they were irresponsible and incompetent. It made you feel afraid and unsafe all the time. You felt lonely and unloved. You thought that you must have been a bad person to be treated that way, and you thought you were unlovable because you didn't get enough love. But you must understand that you weren't bad at all. You were just in the hands of the wrong people. You weren't loved enough, not because you are unlovable but because those people couldn't love or show love properly. So, it is their fault, not yours.

Your stepfather did those horrid things to you not because you are bad but because he is a very sick person. If he had been found out, he would have been locked up in prison or in a mental home. That is where he belongs.

Mother didn't rescue you, and she left you alone with him, because she didn't know what was happening. You wonder why she married such a sick person who drank all the time. She was weak and unhappy and was just desperate to have someone there, even though he was so awful. She felt that she didn't deserve to have a nice man because she was too insecure. Mother was so wrapped up in her own problems that she neglected you. She could barely look after herself properly, let alone you as well. You feel sad because she always sent you away to other people. You feel rejected and unloved. Mother hadn't got much love for herself, so she couldn't give much to you. If you had been very poor, and your mother had very little food for herself, she wouldn't be able to give you much either, because there wouldn't be enough to go round. Love is a bit like that. She didn't reject you because of you; she did it because of herself.

Because of what your stepfather did to you, you feel bad

and guilty. When a grown-up abuses a child in that way, it makes the child feel guilty. *He* made you feel guilty. If someone hit you and stole something from you you'd feel all sorts of emotions. You'd feel angry, frightened, revengeful, hurt, sad and vulnerable. If a grown-up sexually abuses you, you feel all those things except that you feel ashamed and guilty too. That is because it is happening to your body and because it feels so horrible, but you can't stop it. He told you to keep it secret, but that didn't mean you were bad. It was *his* secret you were keeping. He wanted you to keep it secret so that *he* wouldn't go to prison. He knew he was to blame, but he also knew that you would feel it was your fault, so you'd be too scared to tell. He was sly and took advantage of you because he could see that your mummy wasn't close to you and you didn't feel comfortable talking to her.

Today you are still hurting because of other people and what they did to you. You feel lonely because you can't trust anyone. But I am here now and I'm going to help you to get better. I want you to be happy and safe, but you will have to feel the hurt of what happened until you don't feel it any more and I will protect you and comfort you. No one will hurt you now, because I won't let them. I know you are always searching for someone to take care of you permanently, because you have never had that and miss it terribly. You are very needy. We do have people who care, but people aren't forever. When there's nobody else, I am here—and, unlike other people, I am always here. I am your safety net. The hurt will heal eventually. All this pain belongs to the people who hurt you. You are separate and different from them. That is why you felt so lonely—because you weren't part of them. That means that you are a normal, healthy girl and we can make a good life for ourselves.

Below is another letter from Richard to his 'child'. He explains why the child did the sexual things requested of him by the abuser.

Richard

Dear Richard

I am going to write to you today and try to explain a part of human nature to you. In fact it is not just human nature—it is something that is part of all living things. It is the will to survive, no matter what the cost is at the time.

You remember I told you about the fox that gets caught in the trap and how it will chew its foot off to get out? Well, that is the fox's will to survive. It will do whatever it has to at the time to get out of the trap. It was the same with you—you were stuck in a trap and the only way out was for you to offer to do things to please Aunt Ellen. But, unlike the fox, no matter what you did, for you there was no way out. Because whatever you did just made the trap get tighter. You were not to know that—you were just using your will to survive, by using whatever you could to try and take away some of the pain. So, don't feel guilty about what you did—the will to survive will take over whenever you are placed in any trouble or danger. You will not be able to control it. Even when you get older, the will to survive can take over when you are put in various situations. So never feel ashamed or guilty. Aunt Ellen is the one who should feel guilty—she is the one, not you, who has to justify her actions, because she is the one who started her games. She made sure that you would never win.

Imagine you start to play a game with your brother, James—a game you have never seen played. As you start to play, you have your go first and James says you did that wrong and he has six free goes because you made a mistake. He tells you how you should have done it. After he has his goes, you have yours again. You do it the way he said and again he says you did it wrong and he has another six goes. You would either ask him to explain all the rules before you play any more or you would call him a cheat and walk away. That is the type of game you were playing with Aunt Ellen. She couldn't explain the rules because she made them up as she went along so she would always win. There is no way you could have called her a cheat and walked away—you just had to play the best you could.

Cuddle a Teddy

The second part of comforting the 'child' is a physical one.

When going to bed, or perhaps when feeling particularly weepy and lonely, a Teddy bear or pillow can be used to cuddle. The Teddy or pillow should be held the way a child needs to be held—stroking the Teddy as one would stroke a child's hair; rocking and comforting as the 'child' needed to be rocked and comforted so many years ago; speaking to the 'child', either in thought, in a whisper or aloud, telling her the kind of things written in the letters. This exercise is particularly helpful when feeling a need to be cuddled and no relief can be found through being cuddled by a partner. The problem is that the 'child' needs the cuddle, not the 'adult' woman at that time.

For this exercise, address the Teddy as though it were the 'child'. Some clients have even made large rag dolls which resemble themselves as children to do this exercise with.

What Does the 'Child' Feel?

Once contact has been made with the 'child' and she has been given information, support and love, it is time to ask the 'child' to tell about her feelings. That may sound quite a bizarre thing to suggest, and most of my clients look a bit taken aback at this suggestion. However, the results of this exercise can be very surprising.

First, start the letter by asking the 'child' to tell about the traumatic event. For instance, 'Remember when Uncle Harry took you to the shed by the rubbish dump? Please tell me about what you remember and how you felt then. I know this will be hard to do, but I shall be here with you and you can stop any time you need to.' Then, leaving a bit of space on the paper between writings, let the 'child' write and tell about it. This gives the 'child' the opportunity to release the painful event and to expel some feelings to someone who cares. You may have to write from the adult's conscious memory at first, but the 'child' memory will slowly begin to take over. For some people this takes a few paragraphs; for others a few letters. It may be found that, when writing as the 'child', the handwriting becomes more childish or spelling changes. That only means that the 'child' is surfacing and the feelings are strong. The 'child' may also remember some things that the adult memory had forgotten.

When the 'child' has finished writing, she should be praised and thanked for being so brave to face the frightening memories. Again, just leave a bit of space on the paper between the 'child' and 'adult' writings and say something to the effect of, 'Thank you so much for telling me about those things. I know how hard it was for you, and you are very brave to face it. It is all out in the open now and I will be able to help you understand and overcome the pain it has caused you.'

It also helps to draw a picture of the traumatic event. This assists by taking the picture out of the mind and putting it on to paper. It can be imagined leaving the mind and travelling through the pencil.

Below are some samples of letters to (in *italics*) and from the 'child', drawings and an example of how handwriting changes. The first example, from Katy, also includes the letter back to the child giving information, support and love about the specific event, which is part of a series of letter exchanges explained at the end of these samples.

Katy

Dear Child

I am going to ask you to write down some of the things that happened with your stepfather. It will be scary and you'll feel bad, but it is important because it will help you to get better. When you do it, you'll get many bad feelings, but these are harmless. It won't harm you to hurt. Writing it and feeling it means healing it. As you remember what happened you'll feel guilty even though it wasn't your fault. You won't always feel like that. He is guilty for what happened and totally responsible. Remember that everything he did was his fault. He initiated it. Remember that anything you felt or did or didn't do was just a response to what he did. You were too little to know what was happening and what to do about it. Don't blame yourself. He had the responsibility and the power, and whatever you did or felt was only a response to what was done to you. Everything you feel now is because of what he did. Don't worry about telling, because it's not your secret you are keeping—it's his.

The first time it happened I was nearly six. Then when I was seven they got married and we moved to Stratford. He didn't do anything to me for a long while. He went to work. One day, he brought home a puppy for me. When I was eight, during the summer, it started again. I had come home from school and as usual he was sitting on the settee under the window, reading the paper quietly. I had become used to seeing him there. I had forgotten about the abuse that happened earlier. Because I was in a happy mood on this day, when I got home I rushed up to him and said 'Hello, Daddy,' then hugged him. He returned the hug. It was a nice feeling and new because mum never hugged. She was always silent and cold. Her face was always tight-lipped, so I felt that I had to keep back from her.

After a while of cuddling, he started touching me. I froze. It felt as if it had happened before—it seemed familiar. He carried on for some time, and I couldn't move.

He wasn't working any more, so, when I got up in the mornings, mum would be gone and he would be in bed in the sitting-room. He'd have his pyjama pants down and be touching himself. He said to go in bed with him, but I stood there petrified. But he kept on saying it over and over again. It got on my nerves. Then I'd be standing near the bed. He'd keep on asking me to take my undies off, but I just stood there frozen. He kept saying 'Don't be shy.'

Then I'd be in the bed and he'd touch me. The first time it happened like that he tried to kiss me, but I pulled back in revulsion. I didn't like his face and pulled away from it. When this all happened, I felt like I was in a different world. It was weird and sickly. Afterwards I'd try to forget it ever happened, but I never trusted him or went near him.

During the day when we were alone in the house, he kept taking his trousers down and touching himself in front of me. That's all he ever seemed to be doing. Sometimes he'd take me down to the off-licence for his drinks, then when we got back home he'd start doing it again. I never knew what to do. I just stood there. I kept wishing he'd stop it, because it made me feel so awful. I'd be so scared my arms and legs would ache and then I'd go numb and feel strange.

Sometimes, when he'd be abusing me, I would think of the

children at school and feel miles apart from them. I thought
I was a very bad, evil person. When I was with other
children, I felt that they were so innocent and I was so
deceitful. I felt like the wolf dressed up as a lamb in that
story.

*Thank you for telling me those things. Don't blame yourself for
how you reacted. You were too small to know what to do and
you were muddled. That's a very scary thing to happen to a
little girl, so it was normal for you to be frightened and
confused. All those feelings were because you felt frightened
and powerless. Because you were frightened, you couldn't
move or walk away. Because he was a grown-up and kept
asking you those things over and over again, you felt as if you
had to do it. Because you didn't have any attention or love
shown to you, it made you feel like you have to please people.
You wanted to be liked. You wanted cuddles like any child
does, but you didn't want the bad parts.*

*He was very sly and he knew how vulnerable you were. He
knew that if he was nice to you and kept asking like that, you
would feel obliged to do what he asked. He was using 'niceness'
to manipulate you because you are a good girl and like to
please people. That's because you want to be liked.*

*But now it's all over. That will never happen to you again.
You don't have to do anything for anybody. You can say 'No'
even if someone is being 'nice'. You don't owe anyone
anything.*

*You are just as good as the children in your class. Abuse
happens to many other children too. There were probably other
children there it was happening to as well. Remember your
friend Karla, and how she used to go very quiet when you
mentioned her father? She said she didn't like him. Remember,
you felt that he was abusing her? Well, he probably was. But
Karla wasn't nasty or dirty—she didn't seem different—just
like you aren't nasty either. You were a normal, good little girl
and you reacted quite normally in the circumstances. He was
the wolf in lamb's clothes. He was deceitful. He was evil and
dirty and nasty. But because he involved you, he made you feel
that you were bad. That's how Karla must have felt, too.*

He didn't abuse you because of something to do with you. He did it because he was sick. But it's not a sickness of the body that you can see: it's a sickness inside his head that you can't see. That's why he did those things. Remember when you used to go over to Uncle Bill's? He never did things like that. That's because he was a normal person. When you were being abused, you used to feel that you were bad like your stepfather. But you weren't. You only felt bad because of all the horrid feelings you had, because of the 'badness' that he put inside you.

Those feelings are a response to what happened to you and they will go away as you get better. There was no way you could have stopped it from happening. Many children are abused, and they can't stop it from happening. They are trapped like you were. You didn't know about things like that—about defending yourself and saying 'No'—because your mother didn't ever talk to you. Nobody told you what you should do if such a thing happened. So it wasn't your fault at all. You were just as 'innocent' as the other children.

I will look after you now and I won't let anyone do anything to you that you don't like. I promise you this.

The next example is from Sonja, who at twenty-seven years old had the first memory release about the sexual abuse she had repressed the memory of from her childhood.

Sonja
This letter is about the hardest thing I have ever had to do. It has made me come face to face with a reality that happened nineteen years ago, the memory completely blocked out until a few days ago. I was eight years old at the time. Sonja, can you tell me about what happened to you in the shed?

I'm playing in the shed with my two favourite dolls and a pretend dog called Toby. The shed is lovely and cosy. My sister and I painted it, and mum put up some curtains.

Suddenly at the door stands Uncle Jack. He's got that horrible cigarette in his mouth and I can't hear what he's saying. He's playing with my toys and my hair in bunches. He's pulling me up on to his lap and starts to cuddle me and tickle me. I don't like it, but he won't stop. He's pulling my pants down and touching my bottom. I'm going to tell

mummy, but he won't let go of me and says mum knows he's
here and it's all right. But it isn't.

   He undoes his trousers and, oh no, he's making me touch
him! I don't want to but he's holding my hands there. I'm
scared . . . what's happening? He's pulling me close and it
hurts. Please stop . . . oh no . . . Mummy . . . He says
mummy will be cross with me if I tell her, so I had better be a
good girl. I'm hurting and I'm scared . . . oh help me . . .

My bottom's sore and I'm cold, but Uncle Jack is still here. He makes me touch him again and puts it in my mouth. I can't breathe . . . I feel sick. He's making me suck him. Uncle Jack is making noises. I'm scared but he won't let me go. I've got to swallow all this stuff, he's making me. I feel horrible . . . I can't breathe . . . I'm scared.

I'm all slimy . . . Uncle Jack's done that. Now he's licking me all over. I don't like it, go away, go away! I hurt . . . where's my sister? . . . I'm scared.

Well done. I know you must have found that very hard to do, but you said it. It's all out in the open now, so I can help you and be by your side. I'll always be there, so don't worry. It will never happen again. Now, we have to start to make things better—but don't worry, I'm here now. We're in this together, and together we'll win through all this and survive.'

On p. 63 is an example of how handwriting and spelling can change when the 'child' emerges.

Explain the Traumatic Event

After the 'child' has told about a painful event, it is time to write back and explain the event to her. The 'child' needs to know that she was not guilty, that she could not stop or prevent the abuse and that she should have been protected by the adults, not victimised by them. Explain that what the adult did was wrong, give an example of what should have happened (healthy behaviour) and assure the child that you will help her understand and that you love her—in other words, give information, support and love.

Remember that the letters *to* the 'child' need to be repeated until both 'child' and 'adult' fully believe the information. Do not worry if at first the information sounds 'wooden' or less 'natural' than you would like—early letters in the series will be like that, but it does not alter their effectiveness. The correct information does eventually get through and become a sound belief of both 'child' and 'adult'.

Overleaf is a sample letter explaining the painful event to the 'child'.

Richard

Dear Richard
I have got such a lot to write about today that it is hard to know where to start, so let us take it one step at a time. I want to try and explain why Aunt Ellen did some of those things to you. I know adults are hard people to understand, but as you get older, with my help, I hope things will become clearer and I hope I will be able to show you that not all people are like Aunt Ellen.

I want you to think about the first time she called you into the bathroom and you saw her with no clothes on and how she mocked you for blushing and being shocked. No wonder you felt that way. If you had a sister then you would have known what a girl looked like under her clothes—you would have seen her have her nappy changed or, if she had been about your age, you may even have had a bath with her and because you would have been the same age there would have been nothing wrong in that at all. The thing that was wrong when you had a bath with Aunt Ellen was she was using you to make herself feel powerful. That is why she would sit and stare at you when you undressed or when she told you to wash between your legs. It gave her power over you, but remember that not all people are the same and not everybody wants to use you. When you grow up there will be times when someone you love and care for will want to see you undress—not because she wants to use you or be powerful over you but because she wants to enjoy your nakedness, as you will enjoy hers.

Do you remember when Aunt Ellen would make you sit and read and how much you hated it, but now that you know how to read and you understand what you are reading you have started to enjoy it? It is the same with most things. Once you understand it, you start to enjoy it.

Now I want you to remember all those times she would make you help her undress and how you tried not to touch her, and if you didn't touch her she would punish you or make you take something else off. The reason she would make you touch her is because it gave her pleasure. She wasn't bothered if you enjoyed it or not—she was only

thinking about her own pleasure. Another way she got pleasure was the fact she knew she had you trapped—if you didn't do things the way she wanted or if you said you didn't like it, she would punish and threaten you. Think about how you felt when she told you to give her a cuddle. She would never ask if you wanted one, she *told* you. She knew you wouldn't dare say 'No'—she had you trapped. That was the first part of her pleasure. Then when you were on her knee she would touch you, or if you sat beside her she would *tell* you to touch her. That was the second part of her pleasure. It was the same as when you were *told* to sleep in her bed and she would have a nightmare—she said you *must* give her a cuddle and rub her tummy. She was getting her pleasure, but you were never given a choice.

Do you remember in my last letter I told you how touching can bring so much pleasure if it is done with someone you love? Well, when you are older and you feel you want to touch someone then do it. You won't be trapped. Nobody will be saying 'Do this, do that, touch me there or else'—you will do it because you want to, and you will be the one that is in control. It will be up to you to decide who to touch and who you want to touch you, and you will do it because you love the person you are with.

I wish I could take you in my arms right now and give you a cuddle that is given out of pure love. You wouldn't feel trapped—you would just feel loved and protected, and from now on that is what you will be. I will always be here protecting and guiding but, most of all, loving you.

Sylvia has written to her 'child' to explain that she has a right to show feelings:

Sylvia

Dear Little Girl

Do you remember when you were little and everything you did seemed to be wrong? If you laughed it was either too loud, sounded silly or wasn't ladylike. If you cried, you were being naughty, making a fuss about nothing, being ungrateful or just being a pest—which was probably the worst feeling. You were taught that you had no rights and therefore had no right to get angry, and when you did the repercussions were such that you learned that it wasn't worth it.

You very quickly learned that the less you showed emotions and did anything to attract attention, the better it was for you. You became like one of those waxworks, or better still a dummy. Your limbs and mouth moved but you had somehow taught your face and voice to be expressionless.

Do you remember watching other children laughing and enjoying themselves, and wishing you could do the same but not being able to? The only emotion that you really felt much of was sadness. That, dear child, is the one which a little girl should know little of. You were sad and I believe mourning for the childhood lost, the happiness and security that were not yours, the spontaneity that comes from every happy child (even when cross), and the death of a character—yours.

They were so very wrong to make you feel so self-conscious that, consequently, you became a robot. One of the nicest things about children is their spontaneity, and they stole that from you. I bet you looked lovely when you had a smile on your face or laughed. It wouldn't have sounded silly—I would have liked to have heard it.

Everyone has a right to cry—it's one of the first things a baby learns to do. You had the right; you are a person. You were so sure that you were different and didn't have the same rights as everyone else. For many years you even doubted your birth and believed you had been manufactured for the benefit of everyone else. You felt less than a well-trained dog, and a dog never bites its master. But to get good responses, a master is good to his dog and rewards him for being good. You didn't get the rewards.

All emotions are normal—the body needs them to keep well. Your parents were wrong not to allow you yours. If they had, you wouldn't have spent so many years in the mess you were in. It's not that you didn't have feelings—you just buried them so deep that they ate away at you, instead of letting them out in the natural way. In fact, it is almost like you denied yourself anything that was natural, except perhaps eating, which you needed to survive. That you did to excess.

As for anger, you have more than enough right to be angry and you have good reason. You can be angry at your parents because they failed to show you love and protection, at your nana for ignoring what went on, at your abusers for using you, at your uncle for stealing your childhood and innocence, at your teachers for not hearing your cries, and at life for dealing you such a rotten hand. When the abuse turned more frightening and nasty and you felt even more uncomfortable, you again had the right to be angry. I know you felt frightened and you were hurting, but now you can be angry as well, because you know that you have a right. You don't have to accept everything that is dished out to you.

The following letter was written by my client Katy as she was learning where to place the blame for her sexual experiences as a child and how the experiences related to her adult life. The general tone and phrasing of her letter may sound more like a counsellor speaking, but that is to be expected. At first the client needs to 'borrow' the counsellor's words in order to convey the new information to the 'child', but as time goes on that information comes to 'belong' to the client and is related more spontaneously. Katy chose to direct this particular letter to other incest victims. A need to share the new relief-giving information with others in the same boat is a common experience.

Katy

Dear Incest Victim

I want to help you to overcome your guilt because it is guilt that causes you so many problems. It makes you hate yourself and punish yourself. You feel dirty, worthless and damaged. You must remember that you were a victim. You didn't actually do anything wrong—you were done to. The aggressor decided to sexualise the relationship, which was easy because he was in a position of authority over you. He decided to identify your sexuality before you were ready.

Children have pleasant feelings when they touch their genitals. However, this does not mean that they are ready for an adult sexual relationship. They are emotionally and physically immature. Therefore, when the aggressor identifies their sexuality before they are ready it causes severe emotional damage, which affects many areas of their life. How you feel about yourself sexually reflects on your whole life. It colours your perception of everything and affects your relationships with people.

The genitals were designed to give us pleasure. There are

millions of tiny nerve-endings concentrated at the genitals which make them very sensitive. If the genitals are touched, the sensory nerve-endings respond and register pleasure. It is purely mechanical. The genitals will respond to prolonged stimulation whether it is by your own hand, someone else's hand, a penis or a washing machine! Therefore, if an aggressor touches your genitals, they will respond, regardless of your relationship to him. This can make an incest victim feel that her body has betrayed her. If your genitals respond to the touch of an aggressor, it does not mean that you 'asked for it', it does not mean that you are 'evil' or 'dirty' or that you 'enjoyed it'. All it means is that your nerve-endings work and that you are perfectly healthy and normal.

An abusive situation is frightening, deeply disturbing and completely absurd to a child who probably doesn't have the faintest idea what is happening. With this as a background, an abusive situation is obviously not conducive to pleasurable intimacy.

If you had the ability to switch off your nerve-endings, they wouldn't automatically respond and you wouldn't feel guilty. Then you wouldn't feel so terribly confused about yourself and trapped. When a child is subjected to prolonged stimulation, at some point it is inevitable that the child responds to it. This is the 'point of no return' for a child, who then feels completely trapped. It reinforces her determination to keep it a secret. You can't turn your nerve-endings off, it's impossible. So realise that the fact of your genitals responding is purely mechanical and not psychological. Don't blame your body for doing what it's meant to do. Don't feel betrayed by your body. If you hadn't responded then, you wouldn't respond now because that would mean there is something wrong with you physically. Be thankful there isn't.

Because your genitals responded, you may have felt completely confused. You may have felt frightened, sick, angry, guilty, vulnerable, ashamed and humiliated, but you also felt some physical pleasure over which you had no control. And afterwards you may have hated yourself and accused yourself of being dirty and worthless, because in some way you 'enjoyed it'.

But you did *not* enjoy being sexually abused. Consider the fear and confusion—is that enjoyment? Sexual abuse is not something which you enjoyed as a whole experience. It was mainly negative, and what you bitterly perceived as 'enjoyable' was a simple, mechanical response.

Because sexual abuse is something so personal and intimate, you feel deeply invaded. In a normal, loving adult sexual relationship, you can feel complete enjoyment which is totally different from sexual abuse. You feel very close to your partner but in a positive sense, based on trust. You don't feel humiliated and exposed. You let someone inside your heart because it is appropriate and positive. In an abusive situation you are invaded. You do not 'let'. You don't do anything. You are done to. And all the feelings which follow the abuse are purely a response to what was done *to* you. Therefore, you cannot be to blame at all. All your problems, phobias, confusion and guilt are because the aggressor initiated a sexual relationship with you as a child. Even your feelings of deep shame and dirtiness belong to him.

Rescue Scene

After a traumatic event has been disclosed by the 'child' and you have written back to her with information, support and love, it is then time to write a rescue scene—a scene where the adult charges in to stop the abuse and take the 'child' away to a safe and pleasant place. It can also be useful to draw a picture of the rescue scene and another one of the safe and pleasant place.

The abuse will never be forgotten, and no amount of therapy can erase those experiences, but, after writing the rescue scene, the original event will never be thought of without remembering the rescue scene as well. So, although the bad memory cannot be removed, there will be a pleasant memory to soften the pain—a positive memory to leave good feelings: feelings of a conqueror instead of a victim. *The three steps in desensitising painful memories are: writing letters from the 'child' about a specific memory; writing letters of information, support and love to the 'child' about that event; and, finally, writing a rescue scene.*

Below are three examples of rescue scenes.

Richard

I pulled up outside the house, got out of the car and walked to the back door. As I entered the house I was hoping to find them in the lounge so I could just walk in and take him away, but I knew that as Uncle Geoff was at work there would be very little chance of that. I made my way to the foot of the stairs and quietly started to climb them. As I reached the top I could see into the master bedroom. The curtains were drawn but the room was empty. It was then that I heard Aunt Ellen's voice coming from the bathroom. I went towards the door, took a few deep breaths then pushed the door open. It wasn't locked—the bathroom door was never locked.

As soon as I entered, there was an almost overpowering smell of talcum powder, and Aunt Ellen was lying on a towel with Richard kneeling next to her. He turned and looked at me. The look on his face almost prevented me speaking but I managed to say, 'I told you I would come, Richard. Get dressed—it's all over now.' He stood up and ran towards me, arms outstretched and tears filling his eyes. 'I didn't think you were ever going to come,' he said as we hugged each other. It was then that I noticed Aunt Ellen starting to get off the floor. I went over to her and pushed her to the floor and put my foot on her back to prevent her moving. Richard went to his neat pile of clothes and started to dress. I looked down at Aunt Ellen—she didn't even look ashamed. 'No one will ever believe you,' she said, her voice still as sharp as ever, but I wasn't listening.

When Richard was dressed, I told him to pass me the stockings from Aunt Ellen's pile of clothes. I then started to tie her hands behind her back. While I was doing this I told Richard to go and write a quick note to Uncle Geoff telling him what she had been doing. I used her other stocking to tie her feet together. Richard brought his note to me and I added my name and address and said from now on I will look after Richard. I put the note on the window sill, looked down at her and just shook my head—I didn't speak to her at any time.

I took Richard by the hand and started to leave the bathroom. I had only been with him a few minutes, but already I could see a big difference in him. As we left the

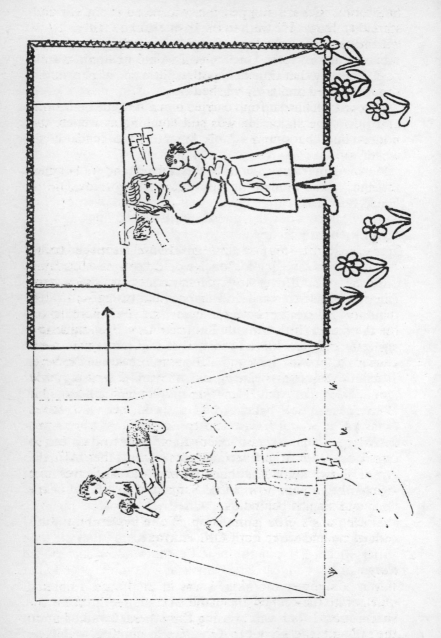

bathroom, Richard stopped me, whispered in my ear and started to laugh. He went to the bath, that was still half-full with water, and turned the taps full on till they jammed. It was now ten o'clock; Uncle Geoff would be home at half past three. By that time her spotless little den of perversion should be well and truly washed-up!

I picked Richard up and carried him out of the bathroom and down the stairs. He was still laughing as we left the house—just the sound of his laughter had made it all worthwhile.

As we drove away, we didn't look back and we laughed together at the thought of Aunt Ellen trying to explain to Uncle Geoff.

Sonja

The scene is set—my cosy little playhouse in the shed being disrupted by Uncle Jack. There he is, cuddling and touching 'little me'. What am I going to do about it before it's too late? Right before he goes any further, I come crashing in through the door. He can't believe his eyes. There he is perched on the floor with 'little me'. Well, I grab his still smouldering cigarette and stub him in the eyes with it. That gives me a chance to pick up 'little me'. 'It's all right now—I'm here. Just hold on—we're getting out of here.' I pick up little Sonja, while red-eyed Uncle Jack is wondering what's hit him. I've spoiled his little game, but we must move quickly—he won't stay placid for long. 'Hold your arms round me, Sonja, and just hold on tight.' We stand up, but so does Uncle Jack. Right, action! I knee him really hard in the groin. Wow, that made him fall backwards! Serves him right—*he's* in pain now. Little Sonja and I rush out of the door and slam it behind us.

Uncle Jack's little game is up. We've beaten him at his own game and we're both OK. Hurrah!

Katy

It was a summer morning. I was in the house. I entered quietly into the kitchen. From there I could see the bed in the sitting-room. John was abusing Katy there. I walked up to the bed and reached out to Katy. 'Come on, Katy—you can

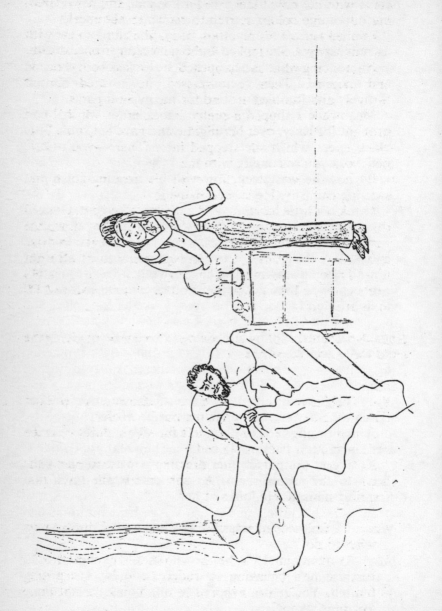

come with me now.' Her face looked pale and bewildered, but now some colour started to return to her cheeks.

I pulled her off his revolting body. She clung to me with tears in her eyes. She looked as though waking from a dream.

On noticing what had happened, he looked both shocked and irritated. Then, embarrassed, he covered himself furtively and fumbled around for his pyjama pants.

Meanwhile I slipped a pretty smock dress, which I had brought for Katy, over her nightie and gave her some little black shoes which she stepped into. 'There—you're safe now, and you're coming with me.'

By now he was struggling with his dressing-gown and swaying clumsily. He looked pathetic.

I took her little hand in mind and we walked out. I locked the door from the outside then dropped the key down the gutter in the street. We got into my car and began to drive away from the house. 'Everything's going to be all right now,' I said. 'You won't ever have to go back there again. No one's going to hurt you again. You're with me now and I'll look after you.'

Katy also wrote the following 'dialogue' rescue scene giving the child the power to escape.

Katy
Katy is eight years old. I am her guardian and can read her thoughts. She sees and hears me but he doesn't.

It is morning. Mother has left for work. John is in the sitting-room in the double bed.

Katy gets up, puts on her dressing-gown and opens the door to the sitting-room. As she enters, she finds him fondling himself. He looks at her.

Katy: I feel so embarrassed and exposed. I don't know what to do.
Me: Look at him. He's the one who should be embarrassed because he's behaving so rudely, and he is exposing himself. You're not exposed at all. You have not done anything wrong.
John: Why don't you come over here?

Katy freezes. Her heart starts to race and she begins to panic. Her arms and legs and tummy hurt and she feels sick and faint.

Katy: I'm scared, but all he wants me to do is go to him, so why am I so scared?

Me: He's manipulating you. What he is doing right now is very wrong and, inside yourself, you can feel that and that is why you're scared. He is a big grown-up and he is bullying you. You must trust your own feelings. If it feels wrong, then it is wrong. Your feelings tell the truth.

Katy: But he only wants to touch me.

Me: It is very wrong for a grown-up to do that. You are too little for that. That is why you feel so bad. Only grown-ups should touch each other in that way. It hurts a child for that to happen to them. It hurts you inside, where it doesn't show. He shouldn't be doing it. He is hurting you by doing it.

Katy: But he is only talking to me, and I feel so scared. Why does that happen?

Me: You're scared because what he is doing is very wrong and you can sense it, inside. He is using words and his body and touching in a way to frighten you. When you feel so frightened it makes you feel powerless. That makes you think that you can't control what happens. He is trying to take your power away from you and he is doing that by frightening you in this way, then taking control of the situation. That is how he hurts you. He does it to make himself feel powerful. He likes it when you feel like this. Right now, while you are feeling scared and powerless, he is feeling powerful and in control. But it is only a trick. He has tricked you into thinking that you haven't any power. but you have, and you can use it.

John: Come on, don't be shy.

Katy: His voice gets on my nerves—it irritates me. I want him to shut up.

Me: That is anger stirring. That is good. Your anger is your power. Let it come to the surface. If you become angry, you'll feel less afraid. Be angry and throw off his manipulative behaviour. You are not really trapped. You only *think* you are. Realise that your feelings are just a normal reaction to what he is doing to you. Even though he might appear to be harmless, he is actually doing quite a lot to hurt you. Realise that you have power and he has no hold on you. Be yourself. Say 'No.' You take control.

Katy: No! I won't do it! I hate you! I'll never do anything you say. You're dirty and horrible and I'm going to tell mummy.

Katy walks away.

Me: Good girl! He won't bother you again, because he is too scared to do it now. He was only doing it when he thought he could safely get away with it. It was *his* secret, not yours, because you didn't do anything wrong. He wanted to keep it a secret so that *he* wouldn't get into trouble. Now, whenever anyone asks you to do something and it feels funny inside—say 'No!' You don't have to do something just because someone tells you to. You can say 'No,' even when someone is being nice and polite. You don't owe them any explanation either. You don't even have to know the reason for saying 'No.' Your feelings are enough to tell you right or wrong. Trust them.

Sylvia's Story

While reading the details of different people's stories, it may have been shocking and anger-making to know that children have experienced these things, that parents and trusted adults can betray children in such a manner. It may have been necessary to set this book aside for a time to regain composure. If that has been the case, preparation may be needed before reading Sylvia's story.

I feel that it is important to include the details of Sylvia's story for the sake of others who have experienced something similar—otherwise they may feel they are not able to be helped because their experiences are much worse than those that we have discussed so far.

Sylvia was six or seven years old at the time of the event her letter describes. She was abused from the age of three to her mid-teens by multiple aggressors, the most frequent being the uncle in this letter. This scene of abuse is different because it involves a man and a woman aggressor, bondage and torture.

Sylvia has very courageously released this most painful disclosure to be used in this book so that others can benefit from it. She felt for many years that no one could help her because the abusive events of her childhood were too many and too gruesome. She now wants others to know that that is not true: the abusive events of childhood *can* be faced and coped with.

Note The events in Sylvia's disclosure are certainly not the most gruesome that children can experience—they only represent the extent of abuse I will deal with in this book. The most common abuse scenarios I have dealt with in my practice are male relative abusing a female or male child, followed by multiple abusers of a female or male child, mother abuser of a female or male child and, lastly, multiple abusers involved in bizarre, ritualised abuse of female or male children. Children used in child pornography rings, child-sexual-abuse rings and witchcraft-based sexual rituals experience the most gruesome forms of child sexual abuse.

Sylvia

Dear Penny

Somehow it seems important to now get it out of my system for good. I can't keep walking around carrying it and thinking about it—it's got to get out of the way of my life. Somehow it will put a 'closed' stamp on it knowing that I have shared it. The things that I am about to write to you come from my adult memory, not the 'child'. I have to take over from her because she becomes so distressed. The details I will describe offend us both—perhaps it is a way of the 'adult' me protecting the 'child', I don't know. Up to now I have not been able to share the actual acts or things that were said, and I still couldn't talk face to face with you about them in detail. I have no wish to be pornographic or to offend, but it seems to need to get out of my system. Maybe writing it may be enough to break its hold on me.

I don't know the correct words for certain acts, even now, but I can remember only too clearly the sort of things that went on and how terrifying it was to me then, and now. I can remember one incident very clearly and can even recently remember how I arrived there. I walked in there, by my own steam, on my own, God help me! Why I didn't stay indoors or tell someone, I have no idea.

I can remember my uncle undressing me and laying me on the table. It was very cold. It had mosaic on top made of tiles and was not as far off the ground as usual—I suppose it was like a coffee-table. I don't remember struggling when they put the straps on me, I don't know why. I should have been scared, but the tying up didn't bother me. What went on after did, however. My uncle and his girl-friend were both playing around with my body with their hands at first, and then would use anything and everything handy to shove up or down one of my body orifices. Sometimes they would put a cushion under me or untie my feet and bend them up to what seemed like my ears—I imagine the purpose being an easier access. I can remember thinking it was like getting ready to do a backward roll. They used cream and things when they did anything—I suppose it was easier to get penetration that way.

They would leave a lighted candle in my vagina, and occasionally the hot wax would drip on to my leg at the very top. I remember I would wake up in my bed the next morning and look for the wax—or rather feel for it to pick it off—but of course it was never there. I was often uncomfortable the next day and got bad pains in my tummy regularly. No one took any notice.

They seemed to take it in turns, which end of me they would use. Sometimes she would crouch astride my face and ask me to suck or blow or lick and he would be up the other end putting himself or something else into me. Sometimes it felt like my mouth, my bottom and my vagina were all full up at once—even my ears were full of their voices or laughter. She would ask me to take her nipple into my mouth like a baby. I knew I wasn't a baby—my little sister did that; I didn't want to. Sometimes they would change ends and he would put his penis down my throat or masturbate over my face. She would be doing other things, like sucking at me while putting things into me. Sometimes she would stand back and watch him and encourage him to do things.

One of the most painful things was when they put a tube into me and cold water seemed to fill me up. I really needed desperately to pass urine but didn't want to because I was too big to do that. Of course, finally I did and I can remember my shame.

He was hairy, and now I think that's why I don't like hairy men. Sometimes I was sick and it would all sort of lie around my ears—it sort of coughed up. It is a wonder I never choked, but I don't think they would have noticed—they seemed far gone somehow. It's funny, but I don't remember them touching each other.

There are so many questions I have that I suppose I'll never be able to answer. What did they do it for? Where were my parents, brother, sister, nanny? How did I get home afterwards? Why didn't anyone see an injury? There was blood—what about when my underwear was washed? Is my uncle still doing it to other children?

It seemed that they just wanted to make me feel so worthless—even to the point of urinating on me. One shouldn't ask 'Why me?' but I don't believe people with a history like mine—of abuse, lack of love and all the rest—can do anything else. It makes you feel that you have to know why life keeps making you the victim.

Emotional Abuse

Some people have felt that emotional abuse is not as bad as sexual or physical abuse. The three are different, but they share the same damaging effects. When trust between child and parent is broken, damage to the child's emotional health is the result. For instance, the child has to trust the adult to explain sexual issues for her (or indeed any issue dealing with her self-image). If trust has been broken, the child is left isolated to come to her own (usually erroneous) conclusions. Therefore, even when sexual abuse has not occurred, a child's sexual identity can be damaged by emotional abuse concerning a sexual issue.

The following series of letters came from a client who 'only' suffered emotional abuse. Notice how the feelings and damaging conclusions drawn by the young girl are very similar to those of her 'sexual and physical abuse' counterparts. I have included the whole series of letters (from the 'child', to the 'child' and the rescue scene) because they are perfect examples of how the letters should be done.

These letters deal with an experience Anne had with her mother. The authoritarian atmosphere of the home and the emphasis put on keeping up appearances was quite restricting for anyone's development as an individual. On this first (remembered) occasion when Anne was almost accidentally able to 'be herself', the rug was cruelly pulled out from under her wobbly self-esteem. The damage was not repaired for many years to come.

Anne's letter from her 'child'

Dear Anne

Remember the school fête and what happened there? Please tell me again what happened and how you felt about it.

I am twelve years old. I am going to the school fête. There are booths and stalls—the tombola stall and the coconut shy. (I haven't seen many coconuts before and I like their brown hairiness, but the milk tastes dusty somehow. The white flesh is lovely, though.) There are games and betting-booths and prizes to be won. The stalls are made from scaffolding and black tarred canvas. It's a warm afternoon and the dust from so many people trampling over the hard, dry earth hangs hazily in the air.

I feel happy. I like the smell of the dusty air and the noises of the fête. People are having fun and laughing. People are buying bargains and making jokes and saying things like 'What the hell—it's all in a good cause' as they eat cake, shy balls, have another go, indulge, make fools of themselves and generally let their hair down.

I am wearing a new dress—I made it myself. My mother says it's 'salmon pink', and it has polka dots and a sash tied in a bow. I had some help to make it, but I did most of it myself and I think I look pretty. I feel shy a little, but good too.

The afternoon draws on and everyone gets ready for the

barbecue and dance. The music is set up and the records are played. People start to dance. They are doing rock and roll. I watch the dancers. The girls twirl around and there is a flash of petticoats. I have a net petticoat too—it has tape at the end and is stiffly starched. I love it.

A boy comes up to me. 'Hey, Blondie!' he shouts, 'D'ya wanna dance?' I am aware that his accent is common, and I am shy. I don't know how to say 'No,' so I go onto the dance floor and start to dance. I have never danced before and I am shy and stiff and awkward. My partner is enthusiastic and encouraging. I think I don't mind being called 'Blondie' after all. I also think 'What the hell—it's in a good cause.'

Infected by the openness and relaxation of the afternoon, I start to relax and enjoy the dance. I try to feel the rhythm and to move as the other dancers are moving. I turn and spin and my skirt swings and my petticoats flash. I am like the grown-ups and a strange boy has asked me to dance. I feel attractive and sophisticated.

Suddenly my mother comes up and hauls me off the dance-floor. Her face is contorted with anger, and I am frozen in shame and horror. I am humiliated in front of a fête full of people. She marches me off to the car and we drive home. She shouts and shouts and shouts: 'You looked so *cheap*!', 'I'm so ashamed. . .', 'Your father's position. . .', 'People like us. . .', 'You've let us down. . .', 'How dare you. . .', 'What do you think you're doing?' and on and on.

I sit frozen in the back seat. Every time she turns to shout at me accusingly or in emphasis of some point of social solecism, she slows the car down and I wonder numbly how long it will take to get home and how much longer I have to endure it all. My silence goads her to greater excesses of anger and malice. It's like the Arabian 'death from a thousand cuts'.

By the time we get home and I can escape to my room I have been well and truly minced. I am devastated by humiliation and shame. What did everyone think when my mother dragged me off the floor? I never said anything to the boy—not thank you, nor goodbye. I had felt so good one moment and so bad the next. So grown-up and confident one moment and so small and shamed the next.

I feel so confused. I saw grown-ups relaxed and letting their hair down for a laugh (even doctors like my father)— why couldn't I do the same? My mother never said *they* were wrong or forgetting their 'positions'. I didn't think I was doing anything wrong or bad, but my mother's rage is huge. She says I'm cheap. Why did my school put up a dance-floor and rock and roll music if it is wrong and bad and cheap and you shouldn't do it? Who is right?

I feel so bad, so very bad. I liked the boy in spite of his accent. I didn't think he was bad. He seemed nice and kind—and we were having a happy time. My mother thinks he's bad, and common and cheap too. I'm cheap. I liked him. I think I'll never be good enough for nice people with nice accents. I'll always be shy and awkward. I'll never really fit in.

Thank you for telling me about this sad incident. I am so sorry it happened to you and that I wasn't there to help you at that time. But I am here now and I will help you to sort out your feelings and to understand who was wrong and why.

Letters from the 'child' are not always pure 'child'—some words or phrases may sound more adult. This is not unusual. At first the letters from the 'child' may be very adult-like, but keep persevering—they will get better. Likewise the letters from the adult may be too adult-sounding for the age of the 'child' in the traumatic events you are addressing. It is useful to check your letters to the 'child' over to be sure that you are addressing her appropriately for her age at the time. However, the occasional inappropriate phrase or word will not jeopardise the effectiveness of the letters.

Anne's letter from the adult to the 'child'

Dear Anne

I was so touched by your description of the school fête incident. You must have felt so very humiliated to be treated like that in front of everybody—ignominiously dragged off the dance-floor in the middle of the dance—then very confused when your behaviour was held to be bad but was no different from anyone else's. Also, the fact of your mother's uncontrolled rage must have made you feel as if you had been especially wicked in some way. Every child in the world would have felt your confusion and hurt, and let me tell you now that you did absolutely *nothing* wrong at all, so don't feel confused or guilty any more. Your mother was completely wrong in her perceptions and her behaviour. Let me explain why and how.

First of all you were right to feel relaxed and happy. It had been a happy afternoon. You looked and felt pretty good. It was a compliment to be asked to dance by a strange boy and gracious of you to accept his somewhat unusual invitation. You were doing a great job overcoming your natural shyness and your conditioned prejudices. You were discovering the joyous freedom and exuberance of dance and that people with different accents and manners can be nice and kind too. Then your mother brutally ended it all.

You were just about to learn that you could be yourself— relaxed, happy, confident—and *still* be appreciated by everyone else. But your mother took that lesson from you and you were forced to endure many shy, painful, priggish 'What will the neighbours think?' comments years before you had the chance to try to be yourself again.

Your mother was wrong—very wrong—hideously wrong —*cripplingly* wrong!! You are not cheap. You are not coarse or common. You are kind and open and generous and joyous. You were discovering new things about the world and the people in it, new things about rhythm and music, new things about yourself and how you fitted in with the world. You copied the adults around you. This is important: it is how we all learn about ourselves and life—there is no other way.

Your mother's view of the world was narrow and snobbish. She was wrong to think that people who didn't have the right accent were somehow bad or 'not nice'. This is called prejudice and has no basis in fact. She was giving you wrong and misleading information. That is why you felt confused. So relax and know that you can trust your own experience and judgement. *Your* feelings and knowledge were accurate, *not* hers.

Your mother was wrong to drag you off the dance-floor in front of everyone else. Even if she thought you looked cheap, she should have waited and unobtrusively called you when the music ended and explained quietly what she thought you were doing wrong. *Her* behaviour was coarse and common in. fact. She shrieked like the fishwife she saw in you and despised in what she perceived as your cheapness. Her behaviour was a grotesque parody of all she purported to loathe in the lower classes. She was an example of how *not* to behave if you wish to be a lady! Her behaviour was brutal and callous. She treated you like some subhuman scum without dignity or feeling. She was a brute and a bully without compassion or control. She was a bad mother and a bad example to you. She was demonstrating adult power over childhood helplessness. You were trapped and forced to endure humiliation and shame. This is bad and wrong. There is no excuse for this behaviour. She should apologise. You are a human being worthy of being treated with courtesy and kindness. You have dignity which must be honoured and recognised. You are learning and might make mistakes. Your mistakes should have been explained kindly and compassionately. You had rights to decent treatment, which were abused. You had feelings that should have been respected but were not.

So be comforted. Your feelings and experiences were accurate. Believe in them and in yourself. I am here to help you to understand that your mother was wrong to do what she did and to free you from your guilt and confusion. You are right to reject her view of the world and to reach out for a freer, wider view of human beings. I love you. Be at peace.

Anne's rescue scene
The dancers move and swirl and rock to the rhythms in the hot dusty evening. 'Hey, Blondie!' a voice yells, 'D'ya wanna dance?' Anne is taken aback and, not knowing how to refuse, shyly steps on to the platform. As the music goes on she relaxes and begins to enjoy herself. She watches the teenagers and adults around her and copies their dance-steps. Her partner is an enthusiastic dancer and pretty soon they are rocking and rolling like the best of them. Anne is

laughing and dancing joyously, free from inhibition and restraint.

Her mother arrives to fetch her and gasps in horror at the vision of her daughter dancing so exuberantly and with someone so obviously 'not out of the top drawer'. Her eyes snap and her mouth purses in rage and resolution. She steps forward, but I grab her arm and hold her back. 'Oh no you don't!' I say firmly. 'You are *not* going to interfere with her. You are *not* going to shame and humiliate her and impose your narrow prejudiced values upon her. You are *not* going to bully and browbeat her into guilt, confusion and inhibition. You can stay and watch her learn about people, social habits, herself, music and dance if you like, or you can get the hell out. But you will not destroy her or touch her.' She shuts her mouth and stumbles away.

I watch Anne dancing and learning and growing up— finding out that common people are not unlike her after all; that she can let her hair down and still be loved; that she can learn to dance and do the things her peers are doing; that boys like her enough to ask her to dance; that she is a competent, likeable, attractive, confident person. She is learning the things she needs in order to grow into a balanced, wise and loving person. When the dances are over, the two of us go to the barbecue area and eat hamburgers with cheese, tomato and lettuce. We drink sweet soft drinks and watch the sun go down and the stars come out in the dark, velvety sky. We talk and laugh and listen to the music and then, together, we go home to bed—tired and happy and deeply contented.

Exact Plan of Action

How, then, can a person stop being made the victim? How can an individual actually use all these exercises? Where does one start?

After I have explained to a new client all the effects that sexual/physical/emotional abuse can have on a person, she is then able to identify her personal list of symptoms as being a result of her damaging childhood. I then ask her to give me a list of the most traumatic memories from her childhood.

There will be obviously damaging memories, but this list may also contain what appear to be fairly ordinary events. The events are secondary; the feelings that the child had about the events are what make them traumatic. This list usually contains from four to eight memories.

I then enquire further, asking if there are any memories connected with shame or blame that are not on the list. A shame memory is one where the child may have felt physical pleasure and consequently responded to the abuser or felt special and important and therefore returned to the abuser. A blame memory is one where the child may have had a chance to tell someone she was being abused, but did not.

If there are any shame or blame memories, I immediately give the client information to help her understand them so that she does not go away feeling exposed or dirty. I explain that any child who responded physically to sexual abuse is simply a child whose genitals worked properly. It does not mean she is bad or dirty, nor does it mean she must have 'wanted' the abuse to happen (two of the most common beliefs of victims). Any child would respond to gentle touch—that is the way our bodies were designed to react. It only means that the child is normal.

Children who felt special and important and returned to the abuser were simply children whose emotional needs were not being met properly. It is parents' responsibility to meet their children's emotional needs appropriately, so that those children will not have to settle for abuse attention.

Blame memories do not indicate a 'bad' child either. Most children sense that the adults around them do not want (nor even know how) to talk about the subject of sex, let alone the subject of sexual abuse within a family. Most children fear that they themselves will be risking prison (at the most) or become a social outcast (at the least) if they disclose sexual abuse. If a child has heard of any other child who disclosed, the subsequent trauma observed following that disclosure would prevent most children from risking the same. A child who does not take the opportunity to tell is simply a child trying to survive—a child trying to protect herself the only way she knows how, by keeping her abuse secret.

The client adds any shame or blame memories to the list and

numbers all these memories in order of severity. If there are five memories, for example, the worst one will be number 5, the easiest number 1. This is where we begin—at number 1.

I start my clients off with a letter to the 'inner child', making contact for the first time—a letter of introduction. The adult gives the child information and support and expresses love. It is basically a letter stating, 'All those things that happened to you were wrong and it was not your fault. I wish I could have been there to save you from that or to help you through it. However, I am here now and we shall work together to solve the problems caused by those events from the past. I will not leave you alone—I will help you understand, heal and go forward because I love you very much.'

Next the 'child' is asked to write about her feelings concerning memory number 1. We are hoping for a letter from the child's point of view, full of the feelings she had then—avoid any temptation to justify the actions of the adults in the memory. This letter should be written in the first person. It may start with information from the adult's conscious memory, but soon the 'child' voice will take over and the words will come very quickly—there will be no time for the adult to stop and think of what to say next. Most clients find this happens the first time, but a few will perhaps need to work through three or four letter attempts before the 'child' speaks freely. Also, remember, it is not surprising for the handwriting to change to a childlike scrawl and for spelling to deteriorate as well. However, the writing does not always change, nor does it make a difference to the effectiveness of the letter if it does not.

After the 'child' has told her side, the adult writes back with a clear explanation of the event, which includes:

1. acknowledging the child's feelings as normal,
2. giving information that the adults in the scene were wrong to have abused her,
3. describing what healthy parenting/behaviour would have been,
4. giving support and love.

For example: 'You were right to feel confused and frightened—*any* child would have felt that way. You were not being disloyal to your father; he was being disloyal to you. It is always the adults' responsibility to see that the behaviour between themselves and children follows proper guidelines. Adults have the power to make sure that proper behaviour happens; children do not. He was wrong to touch you between the legs and make you touch his willy. Your father should have offered you a safe, normal hug—a hug that would have made you feel loved and cared for. The two of you could have sat on the sofa cuddling and enjoying the television programme. Then, when you went to bed, you would not have felt frightened, confused and afraid that it was somehow your fault. If your father had cuddled you properly you would be able to trust and believe him. I wish I could have been there to save you from experiencing all that, to comfort you. But I am here now and we will work together until all these problems are solved. You are a lovely little girl—you deserve much better than what you received back then and I love you very much.'

A couple of letters may have to be written to the 'child' explaining the event before she thoroughly believes the information. I generally ask my client, 'On a scale from 1 to 100%, how much do you believe the information you have given the child?' Clients are soon able to know when their adult 'logic' believes the information but their child 'feelings' do not. If the child's belief is below 80%, I assign more letters.

The rescue scene is next on the agenda. It is the last step to desensitise the memory. The adult must be seen to be the most powerful person in the rescue—no sneaking up the back stairs to take the child away! The adult should burst into the front door like Superman, take control of the situation, comfort the child and then whisk her away to a safe and happy place— never to return to the old scene again. Each rescue scene is separate, because each memory is separate, therefore each time the rescue scene is enacted, as my client goes through her list, it is done as though it had never been done before. Some clients have said 'But I already rescued her once—do I do it again?' The answer is 'Yes.'

Once my client finishes memory number 1, we move on to memory number 2. We continue through the list until it is finished.

Once in a while another memory will surface that my client did not remember previously. Such memories are usually more traumatic than the rest (that is why they were buried), but the experience of settling the other memories normally gives the client courage to face the new one. However, if this process should become too overwhelming while doing it on your own, I suggest involving a therapist or a counsellor to help finish the work (using this book as a guide for them to follow). Desensitising the major memories generally resolves the minor ones as well—it should not be necessary to try to tackle every single bad memory from childhood.

Anger exercises (described in the next chapter) are begun according to my client's need. If she is expressing a lot of anger verbally, we may start off with anger exercises to help release pressure. However, if the anger is buried under a thick layer of control, we may tackle it after (or sometimes during) working on the memories.

Learning assertiveness skills is essential in order to build up the 'adult' identity, to give the 'adult' a voice. These skills can be learned while doing any of the other exercises. It takes time and practice to become assertive—if there are any assertiveness training courses available, take them. Without a strong 'adult' voice and identity it will be difficult to take charge of your life. Assertiveness is an essential tool to have while learning how to stop being made the victim. (Refer to the Book List at the end of the book for recommended assertiveness texts.)

Comparing 'Voices'

Everyone engages in what we call 'self-talk'—it is what we think about during the day or, perhaps more to the point, what we are telling ourselves during our waking hours. If we have a very damaged self-image, our self-talk is usually full of blaming, accusing statements followed by fearful or angry replies.

For most people the everyday phenomenon of self-talk is never really closely examined, or perhaps even acknowledged. However, it is very important to be aware of what our self-talk is saying, because we tend to believe those messages and behave accordingly. For example, if our self-talk is full of name-calling statements whenever we make a mistake ('Stupid! How could you be so clumsy! You stupid fool!'), we believe that we are stupid and a fool—and, what's more, we believe that everyone else believes that too. Even when other people tell us that they do not think we are stupid or a fool, we seldom believe them.

The good news is that damaged self-talk can be changed. The bad news is that changing it does take time and effort—however, it is the most rewarding thing you can do for yourself. It takes time to correct because it has been with you from the beginning—since the adults around you began to use name-calling or blaming or accusing statements to communicate with you. It feels so familiar that it feels 'true', and in fact most of us even try to defend the statements: 'But I am stupid; I do act like a fool.' The truth is, everyone acts foolishly at some time or another, but that is not their entire personality nor is it yours. As long as we believe and repeat negative messages to ourselves, we cannot grow to our full potential.

Our self-talk consists of three 'voices': the Parent voice, the Child voice and the Adult voice. Self-talk is a normal experience that everyone has and should be a very helpful tool to understand life. However, those people who during childhood received negative messages and abusive behaviour from significant adults develop a damaged self-talk. Although their abusive adults are no longer present, their negative statements carry on in the role of a damaged Parent voice.

The Child in our self-talk represents the child we once were. A damaged Child voice responds to the Parent voice fearfully or angrily but consistently with a feeling of guilt.

The Adult voice is non-judgemental and factual. The Adult voice collects information and applies it appropriately to our life experiences. If, however, we have had few healthy Adult role-models, our Adult voice may become ineffective and weak. Each voice has an important role, but the Adult voice should be the executor—the one in charge.

The first step in ridding ourselves of damaged self-talk and replacing it with healthy self-talk is to start listening to what we say to ourselves in our mind whenever something goes wrong. Table 1 gives examples of the kind of messages people hear in their self-talk from the damaged Parent voice, damaged Child voice and ineffective Adult voice. Table 2 gives examples of self-talk messages from the healthy Parent voice, secure Child voice and effective Adult voice.

Table 1 Negative 'self-talk' voices

Damaged Parent voice (accusing, blaming, punishing and name-calling)	Ineffective Adult (ill-informed, un-assertive voice and no control)	Damaged Child voice (fearful, angry and self-sabotage)
Look what you've done now! You ruin everything! I shouldn't expect anything different from you! Did you think you could really do it? You made your bed, now lie in it. You will never be any different. Stupid! Clumsy!	I suppose kids who are abused ask for it—that's what people say. Mum and dad must have been right. Other people know more than me. I don't like what they say, but I can't stop them. I don't know my rights.	I can't, I'm afraid. Don't be angry, I'll do it. I want to hide. I'll get you back! Don't trust anyone! Hurt people before they hurt you! Everyone hates me! I'm bad, dirty, ruined and contaminated, so I deserve it. I'm bad, etc.—I shouldn't be happy.

Table 2 Positive self-talk voices

Healthy Parent voice (teaching, monitoring, acknowledgement; non-judgemental voice tone)	Effective Adult (information-gatherer; strong, assertive voice; strong manager; realistic assessment)	Secure Child voice (spontaneous, creative, curious, fun)
That works like this . . . Give this a try. Here is a good way. This may be useful. Don't forget the keys. It's raining—do you have the umbrella? You have worked hard —well done! You did your best— good effort! You were very assertive —well done!	If I don't know, I shall find out. I enjoy learning. I respect others' rights. I respect my rights. I am responsible for myself. I soon recognise damaged Parent and Child messages and defuse them. I am in charge of my life, and I feel happy and strong in it.	I'll try it! Let's go and see. I've got a good idea to try! Look what I've made [discovered]. Lets see how this works. I want to try this new way. Let's be silly! I like making you laugh. I like laughing.

It is helpful to make a list of the messages normally heard in one's self-talk, to identify which voice they belong to and to deal with them appropriately. Most clients are quite surprised about the number of damaged Parent messages they hear during the course of a day. They realise that their thoughts have become a battle between the damaged Parent and the damaged Child, with the occasional comment from the ineffective Adult—quite a tiring and useless waste of emotional energy. (*Born to Win*, by Muriel James and Dorothy Jongeward, and *Staying OK*, by Amy and Thomas Harris, are two good books explaining the Parent/Child/Adult 'voices'. Refer to the Book List at the end of the book for details.)

7 Guilt and Anger Exercises

Understanding Abuse

Facing and understanding the subject of sexual abuse is the first step to overcoming it. First, victims must know the subject. It is important to read everything they can about the sexual abuse of children and its consequences—about aggressors, mothers, victims, society's attitude and the law. They should try to see the complete jigsaw puzzle instead of just their own small piece in it. There will be case histories much worse than theirs, and some not nearly as bad. Emotions will take a beating—they may have to put a book aside for a while. They will feel anger, bitterness, sadness and probably several more emotions. Their own past will come back in Technicolor as they read, and so may nightmares, but the subject must be faced and understood if it is to be overcome.

Below is a piece written by a client describing her feelings as she began therapy and the frightening task of facing the past.

Sylvia

And so, unearthed is a horror story—or at least to the one concerned. Not so much horror to those who have suffered worse, but still to the victim a disabling, sickening, all-enveloping realisation of one's past. A feeling of little worth, of being used, of helplessness and, yes, self-pity.

The questions come, the whys. The pain of unveiling what has safely been stored and locked away into one's subconscious. Then the fogs, the places that still will not yield to the probings. The hurts that do not bear the fruit and release of tears are locked away there too. The questions are there—even the quizzing of memory: what is truth, what is imagined, how much is just acceptable excuse for one's wanderings, for one's mixed-up grey matter?

Still afraid to tell—even to one's self—and yet what penalty could be inflicted? What harm? Rather a release from the crippling malignancy. A key is needed, a decoder. A need to talk and talk as if it could all be spewed out by mouth, and yet the knowledge that what is so important to one's self would be trivia or a bore to another. There is a need for a kindred soul, a very selfish need that would far outstretch human friendships, time or understanding.

Then there is the family, the rights or wrongs, the betrayal of secrets, of those who tried (maybe misguidedly) to do their best. Those who were beset by their own troubles and probably unaware of damage they were causing to the child. The frustration of not being able to confront the family members to get at their version of the happenings. Aware of the pain it would cause and the barrier already up, the refusal to admit.

So, the question of how much self-indulgence? The knowledge that every moment waking, and often in sleep, is taken up thinking about it. It is all-consuming—nothing else holds its own place anymore. The old roles don't hold up. The days of acting seem to be over and yet nothing solid emerges. There are the days when the 'child' manifests— afraid, wanting love and acceptance, easily hurt. Another when the world is so bleak that despair takes over. Another that is filled with hope. Another when one is so muddled that even day-to-day existence is almost an impossibility. Days when the thought that it is all a lot about nothing, a mountain out of a molehill. Days when communication is easy; days when it is an impossibility.

One wonders how much time can be given to self-indulgence. Thoughts of getting up, shaking and saying 'So what! Let's get on with what we were doing before we opened the chambers of memory.' The question of does one go on or go back to living as before? Should one strive for other than what one is given? The knowledge that one's mind is so tangled that only someone very wise could begin to straighten it. The desire is still somehow there to live a life of peace with one's self and the world. To die knowing that somewhere you have been used for good purpose.

Sheer folly is the thought that it can be all parcelled up

again and be put back into the dark chambers of forgotten memory. Yet what of that which is still hidden—should one pick and probe till all is revealed? Why has the mind closed chambers if not for protection? But, is half the story enough? Can it be lived with or should healing of the damaged emotions be sought? Shall one probe into the depths and hopefully find healing with the full story?

Write a List

Taking in information about sexual abuse helps when coming to terms with guilt. Reading about the many cases of children victimised by trusted adults produces the understanding that only adults are to blame for any sexual activity with children. That fact will not automatically become part of a victim's belief system, however; it must be given some assistance.

First the victim must write a list of reasons why she was blameless as a child. If that is difficult, she may start with some case histories and write the same list on behalf of the child in the story. This will get her mind moving in the right direction and make her own list easier. She should keep the list and add to it if and when she thinks of more reasons—reading the list over to herself when guilt feelings bother her.

It must be remembered that the guilt she felt originated when she was a child, with a child's perception of life, and is based on false assumptions. It is now time to look realistically, as an adult, at what happened. The childhood belief that she is guilty for what some adult chose to do to her is as inappropriate as keeping the childhood belief in Father Christmas.

Anger

Many of my clients have problems coping with the anger in themselves. They can be divided into two groups. The first recognise their anger and may even find that it spills over into other aspects of their lives (taking anger out on children, family, themselves or possessions). The second feel that they have no anger. The truth is that their anger has been repressed for so long that it is not recognisable as such. They are surprised to find out that self-sabotage, illness, phobias, etc.

are in part the manifestation of buried anger. These people usually have a great deal of anger to exorcise once they do get in touch with it.

So many clients say to me, 'I know I shouldn't, but I hate my father [or mother].' It is as though father and mother are gods and to say anything against them is blasphemy. Most people can produce children—that, in itself, warrants no prizes. Being a successful and effective parent is another matter. If your parents were inadequate and betrayed you, you have every reason to feel angry and bitter and to hate them. In fact, it would be a bit strange if you did not.

Some well-meaning people may admonish others not to hate: 'Oh, you should never hate anyone. Just put it out of your mind.' I agree that living with hate as a companion does considerable damage to one's emotional and physical well-being, but to say 'Put it out of your mind' is not enough—it does not work. The following exercises help victims to remove hate and anger from inside and dispose of it in a safe way.

RELEASING ANGER
Using pen and paper, the victim needs to write letters to the aggressor—*but not ones to be posted.* These are just to get the words out of the mind and on to paper—a safe way to release some anger. The letters may be torn up after they have been written, or be saved to look back on later. (If she is working with a therapist, these letters should be taken along to the session and discussed.) The letters need to be very direct—telling the aggressor how the victim feels about what he did to her, and referring to specific events. She should use whatever angry words feel most expressive, not worrying about spelling errors, sentence structure or any other rules. These are for her eyes only (unless she is working with a therapist) and for the sole purpose of expelling anger.

A series of letters should be written until the victim feels that she is no longer 'censoring' her anger and until there is little or no anger left to be expelled. She should write anger letters from her adult feelings and from her 'child' feelings, giving each side full expression. Hopefully, with each letter, the expression of anger is increased to a 'no holds barred' level, allowing the adult and the 'child' to vent angry feelings fully. The adult needs to express anger on behalf of the 'child', and the 'child' needs to express anger until she feels more powerful than the abuser.

The anger need not be limited to feelings towards the aggressor—it should also be directed towards other 'problem people' from childhood. Children perceive the nurturing, protecting role of their mother to be greater than that of their father, so victims can feel as much, or more, anger towards their mother as they do towards the aggressor. Although she may not have participated in the sexual abuse, she was in some way 'not there' for the child—in other words, she was not perceived to be on the child's side and she did not rescue the child.

For the purpose of dispelling anger, the victim must imagine taking all the good points her aggressor/mother had and placing them on an imaginary shelf. With those attributes she loves/likes about the problem person put safely on the shelf, only the person's attributes that she is angry about are left to receive her anger fully. After she has finished the exercise she can put the two sets of attributes back together again. In that way, she does not feel bad about attacking her aggressor/ mother with all her anger, because the part she loves/likes is safe on the shelf.

These letters should not be confined to anger about the sexual abuse—all the hurt and confusion that these problem people may have had a part in should be included. Perhaps a victim was laughed at or called names, belittled or ignored. It should all be written down. (Children seldom suffer sexual abuse, in happy, well-functioning homes.) Nothing should be held back; no one's behaviour excused. It is essential to get anger out of the mind and on to paper, but this cannot be accomplished when trying to go easy on someone. When anger is over with—perhaps for the first time—victims can view these problem people with understanding and calmness. But until anger is expelled the chances of feeling understanding and calm are slim.

Here is a series of anger letters written by a male victim to his aggressor, an aunt. Notice how both 'adult' and 'child' begin to voice their anger in a stronger way as the letters progress. In the final letter there is no question about the 'child' being more powerful than the abuser—in fact the 'child' behaves and speaks with such power that you lose sight of the fact that the 'child' is speaking.

Richard's adult anger letter

Well, bitch, I bet you thought you would never hear from me again—or maybe you hoped you never would.

I have, at long last, told someone about the things that went on when I was '*trusted to your care*'.

I think about you each time a child—molest case is reported, because let's face it, that is what you are—a child-molester. How the hell can you justify what you did? Thirty years after, I am still having problems. I have a wife who I can't stand touching me, I am unable to give all my love to my children and, until I met my wife, I had a drink problem. All this because you had a thing about little boys and spanking. How I would like to get you in that room and have you stand there as helpless as I was, but that would only bring me down to your level and your perverted mind would probably enjoy it anyway.

I hope you don't have grandchildren because I would hate the thought of others going through the same as me, just to satisfy your depraved and unhealthy lustings.

I am 37 now and I am starting to shed my guilt feelings. I now know that it is *you* who is the guilty one. You took my innocence and most of my childhood memories and replaced them with a hate so strong it wouldn't be safe to meet you face to face.

Richard's 'child' anger letter

I am going to start this letter by saying something that so far in my life you have stopped me from saying, and that is '*No*!' That is the answer I want to give to all those questions you ask. When you sit on the side of the bath and say, 'Hasn't auntie got a nice body?' or 'Does that feel nice?' I want to scream '*No*!' so loud that the whole world hears me.

I often picture myself running towards you, as you sit there smiling and staring at me. I picture myself pushing you backwards, shouting '*No*! I hate you!', and I just keep hitting you. I hate the way you stare, I hate your body and I hate you touching me with your bony fingers. You don't treat me like a human, you treat me like a toy.

All I want to do is hurt you. I want to poke you in the eyes when you sit and stare at me, and I would love to bite you hard when you tell me to kiss your body. It would be worth it just to know that I have hurt you as much as you hurt me.

There is nothing nice about you and I don't enjoy the things you do. The only good thing about you is that you are not my mum. I know one day I will be going home. I know that until then you have got me trapped, but while I am doing what you tell me, I picture I am doing what I would really like to do to you. If you knew what I was thinking you wouldn't come within ten miles of me.

I know that you will take no notice of me—you never have—but at least I have told you how I feel, and one day you may be in for a big surprise when my dreams come true.

Richard's later adult anger letter

The first thing I want to know is just who do you think you are? Who gave you the right to play with other people's lives? Maybe you think you are some goddess of love sent to earth to teach us all about love and affection. If that is the case then let me tell you some bad news: you taught me more about hate and disgust than anything else.

Can you think what it was like for me being stuck in the same house as you knowing full well what was going to happen as soon as Uncle Geoff went out? I would dread going in the bath or bed with you. Your touch felt like acid burns and the things you made me do did nothing but complete my hatred for you.

People like you should be put down at birth—that is, if you were born. I get the feeling you were spit up against a wall and hatched, because what you are is lower than the lowest form of life. I can only hope that one day you will be placed in a situation as you had me in, and that there will be no one to come to your rescue, no one that you can turn to.

I don't intend to go through the things you did to me one by one, as they are probably fond memories to a sick mind like yours, but I can still picture your skinny hand reaching towards me. It always reminded me of a spider and the rings you wore were its eyes. Now I have got the power to hurt you. If I was to tell the world what you did, I know I would be believed—but it is too late for all that now.

All I want to say is that the time I was sick over you was the best thing I have ever done. It cost me a good thrashing but it was worth it because that is what you are—a pile of rotting vomit. That is what you were hatched from and that is what you still are.

The final thing I want to say is if you ever come back in another life, for God's sake, marry a midget. That way you can play your perverse little games till your heart is content.

In the 'child' anger letters an element of magic can be introduced, for we want to see the 'child' emerge with feelings of power and a sense of safety. In reality, children are smaller and weaker than adults, so they cannot hit out at them very effectively, but with the assistance of magic they can. In this last anger letter, Richard has given his 'child' the ability to shoot blue bolts of lightning from his fingertips.

Richard's later 'child' anger letter
The time is here again and I can feel her hands starting to touch me. The touch of her hand feels good, but I hate it. I feel like a toy that she has decided she wants to play with for a while and when she has finished she will put me back in the toybox until she wants to get me out again. When she is not playing her games with me, she doesn't even know that I am here.

As always, I pretend to be asleep and hope that she will not try to wake me up, but I feel her getting near to me. I can smell the sickening smell of baby powder she has all over her body and her breath that always smells of peppermint. As her hand starts to undo my pyjamas I can feel the anger building up inside me. No, it is not anger this time, it is something more. I don't have a name for it but it scares me. It scares me so much I must keep it hidden. I cannot let it out because I cannot control it. In my mind I beg her to let me sleep, but she won't and I can feel myself giving in to this feeling. I have controlled it so many times, and for so long, but this time it is in control of me.

I can't even feel her hand now as she tries to remove my nightwear. As she starts to rub her body against me I give in to the scary feeling, letting it take control. She is rubbing against me now but I don't feel it anymore, I am now waiting to take my revenge. As she puts her hand between my legs, there is a flash of lightning. She cries out in pain, pulling her hand out, and there is a burn mark across the palm. She looks at her hand in disbelief, looking towards me for an explanation. But I just look at her and tell her, 'You ask me to do this to you. I tried not to, but you made me. Now you must let me finish.'

I get off the bed and move towards the door, not because I intend to leave but to make sure she can't. She looks at me and gives a pathetic smile. She pats the bed next to her and says, 'Come and lie with auntie.' I am not scared any more as I let the thing inside take over. I point to the spot she is patting. 'You want me *there*?' I scream the word and, as I do, a blue flash leaves my finger and strikes the bed where her hand is. It leaves a mark on her hand but goes through it and on to the bed, making it set alight. She tries to get off the other side, but I again point my finger and again the bed is set alight and every time she moves I trap her in flames. I can see by her face she now knows how it feels to be trapped, and when she thinks there is no way out I put out the flames. She comes forward to thank me but I point my finger at her and tell her to do just as I say or the flames will come back. This scares her even more and she sinks back on to the bed. She is now under my control.

The thing inside me moves towards the bed and auntie backs away from me. When I am in the middle of the bed, I defecate. Then I turn towards her and point to it. 'Everytime I see you, that is all I see. Just something that smells and infects everything around it. But I had to tell you how lovely you were and how nice it was to touch you and I wasn't allowed to be sick or revolted. So now you have to do the same. Stroke it, kiss it, tell it just how lovely it is to hold. Tell it what a nice skin and touch it has, because if you don't then the fire will come back and you don't want that to happen do you?'

She looks at the pile on the bed and then at me. 'You can't

make me. You can't be serious,' she says. 'Why can't I? You made me stroke, touch and kiss something that I thought was just as revolting and I had to pretend I enjoyed it, so now it is your turn.' She puts her hand out to touch it and then tries to pull away, but I shout at her, '*Do it*! Touch it and tell it how you love it!' As I shout at her I point towards her and a blue flash strikes her on her backside. She cries out with pain. 'Do it!' I tell her, and her hand reaches towards it and touches it. There is revulsion and fear on her face. 'Now kiss it and tell it how lovely it is.' She tries to tell me that she can't, but I send another bolt to her backside and she bends to kiss it.

I can see on her face all the feelings that I had when I was made to do the same things to her. At last now she knows just how I felt. I tell her that I can't hear her saying anything. She whispers something, but I still can't hear it, so I aim another bolt at her and it hits its target. I can now hear her telling it how nice it is to touch it and now lovely it feels. She has lost all control now. Scared of my power, she is kissing, stroking and talking to it without direction from me. She is now the one without any dignity or pride.

I aim another bolt at her and she cries out, 'I'm doing as you told me. Why are you hurting me?' I don't reply but I send another bolt towards her. She tries to dodge it but fails, and it strikes her hard. She tries to leave the bed but a bolt from me strikes her on the chest and knocks her back on the bed. She looks so terrified that I know that it is nearly over. I send a bolt towards her crotch and as it strikes it sets fire to her pubic hair. She tries to rub it out but another bolt strikes her backside. Each time I send a bolt the next one gets stronger, leaving a deeper burn mark. The next one I send towards her breast and, as it hits, the breast seems to explode. Another one to her buttocks rips open the flesh—there is no blood, just a gash showing the raw flesh underneath. She is now a quivering heap on the bed. It is time to end it now, I tell her. She tries to beg me not to, but her pain stops her speaking.

Before the final bolt I say to her, 'It's not very nice getting punished for doing things right, is it?' The look on her face tells me she knows just what I mean, but before she can answer I send the final bolt towards her and it strikes her on the temple, making a small hole so it can enter and split her brain. She falls lifeless to the bed, her face next to the pile of defecation. She may have thought it was vile, but it was only another form of what she was. As I leave the bedroom I send a bolt towards the curtains and blankets. She is gone for good.

KILLING THE TORMENTOR

It does not matter if the 'child' kills the tormentor in the letter—that is only an expression of the intensity of the child's anger. It does not mean that the person will have released killer instincts or have exposed a monster—in fact the opposite happens. With the anger finally faced and expelled, the person feels calm and happy, able to deal with everyday anger without a backlog of anger from the past joining in. Sometimes several anger letters will need to be written to each tormentor, or the tormentor may even need to be 'killed off' several times. Clients know when the anger letters are no longer needed, for they are not able to conjure up any more feelings of anger towards the tormentor to put down on paper.

When Richard finished the above series of anger letters, I asked him how much anger, on a scale from 1 to 100, he now felt towards Aunt Ellen. His reply was that he could not even conjure up any anger feelings—he was really empty. If his answer had been more than 20 I would have assigned another anger letter. It is best to conquer at least 80% of the anger before moving on to the next step.

Richard and Katy (whose letters follow shortly) were very worried about the intensity of the anger that came out in the letters. Both were not used to expressing anger in such an undiluted form. Some who have read the letters were also frightened by them, fearing that anger of that nature could be dangerous. It is only dangerous if it is not acknowledged and expelled appropriately. It is dangerous to the person who owns it, for it festers inside and causes emotional damage. It can be dangerous if it is not expelled in a controlled way but instead comes rolling out attached to a different anger source—for example, a similar event in the present stirring up unsettled feelings from the past.

Restricted Anger

People afraid of their anger will often over-control all their emotions. They can appear robot-like to others—never really participating spontaneously in life. Their fear of losing control prohibits them not only from expressing anger but also from expressing and experiencing joy.

Below are three anger letters from a young woman who had been very restricted and over-controlled for many years. Using the anger exercises (both writing and the physical exercises described later) she began to let anger slowly surface until finally she was able to let the full extent of her fury out. The first letter is to her stepfather, who sexually abused her. The second letter is to her uncle, who emotionally abused her with ridicule, humiliation and criticism. The second letter is written in fantasy form, with the wolves representing her anger and their actions representing the intensity of her anger. The third letter is again written to her stepfather. It is also in fantasy form and describes her anger and rage as a creature that her stepfather's abuse brought to life. (Although the second and third pieces are in narrative form and not addressed directly to her uncle or stepfather, they are still considered 'anger letters'. This narrative style should not be used in place of letters addressed directly to the problem person, but it can be useful if used in addition to them.)

After writing these letters she said, amazed, 'I can't believe that all that was inside me. No wonder I've felt so bad all this time!' That statement sums up the purpose of writing anger letters. As long as the angry thoughts are hidden away inside, they are damaging, battering away from the inside; but when expelled, they lose their power. This young woman felt (and behaved) more spontaneously after facing and expelling this anger, for there was nothing left to be kept inside. She could use her emotional energies to live, rather than use them to hide the shame of her intense anger.

Katy's letter to her stepfather
I am writing to tell you how I feel about you. You messed me around when I was a child. Wasn't that easy for you, manipulating a little girl? I suppose it made you feel

powerful at the time, but I know that you were a pathetically inadequate person really. You couldn't socialise and you were always drunk. Your behaviour was ludicrous. You are a joke.

You hurt me as a child, but children grow up. I am now a grown adult, full of anger, hatred and loathing toward you.

When you were abusing me, did you ever wonder what I thought of you? Or did you conveniently switch your mind off? I hated you and despised you. When you lay stretched out on that bed, I was filled with disgust at the sight of you. Your body reminded me of one great writhing, slimy maggot. I loathed the sight of it. When you stretched back like that, I wanted to get a large heavy object and just beat you over and over again and make your body stop moving. I wanted to see you motionless. I wanted to take the life out of that hideous body of yours. But I felt that it would be useless. I thought that if that happened to you, you just wouldn't react. Because, you see, I didn't feel that you were human. I thought that you couldn't feel anything.

I hate you so much, words can't express it. I hate your greasy hair, your slimy face and sickly smile. I hate your mouth, your hands, the way you move. I hate the way you speak. I hate the way you don't speak. I hate the air you breathe and the floor you tread on, and I hate every single atom in your body. To me, you are human refuse. You are worthless, hideous shit. You are worse than anything which might come out of a dog's arse. You are utter, utter filth. You are completely repulsive from the top of your head to the bottom of your shoes. Everything you touch is contaminated and should be destroyed. You are dirt. I don't know why you exist, for you are a waste of space. You are an insult to life. A walking bag of refuse, vomit and dead remains. That is all you are.

For God's sake, do yourself and everyone else a favour—please kill yourself. You should, you know. You are beyond redemption. You are completely degenerate. You are lower than the lowest animal. I would like to kill you slowly. But then you'd be dead and that wouldn't be enough. I'd want to kill you over and over again. I just want you to suffer eternally. I want to stick pins in you and cut you open. I want to pour acid over your vile body and see it disintegrate before my eyes. I want to cripple you and see you bleed until there is no blood left in you. You should be completely taken apart and made to not exist.

But I do not need to punish you, nor do I need to see you go to prison (which is what you deserve), for I know that you are suffering this very minute because you are a miserable, despicable creature. It is enough for me to know that you suffer, and I relish every moment of it. I hate you.

Katy's letter to her uncle

I was nine years old. My mother and I were at Aunt Joan and Uncle Pete's in Leytonstone. Joan was cooking in the kitchen and my mother was talking to her. My cousin, Alan, was looking through a comic, and his sister, Jane, was upstairs in the bedroom. I was in the sitting-room with Uncle Pete.

He sat back in one of the armchairs with a pipe in his mouth, looking smug and smirking at me every now and then. I felt embarrassed because he was behaving so strangely and staring at me as if I were something peculiar under a microscope. He was making an effort to appear to be trying to conceal laughter. Only he did it in an exaggerated way, pulling grotesque faces and giggling at times. I'd had enough.

I rose from my seat and walked right up to him and looked down on him. He looked unsettled and bewildered, because this was not usual, and he tried to remain unruffled. I lashed out from left to right, striking him across the face. His pipe fell to the ground. Suddenly, we were outside on a dusty piece of ground, miles from anywhere, and further on there was a thick forest.

He got to his feet looking around him in horror and amazement. He kept looking around then looking back at me questioningly. 'What happened? Where are we?' I just looked at him hatefully. He said 'What did you do?' and he looked at me fearfully because he doesn't trust anyone. 'I'm going to teach you a lesson, you revolting piece of dirt!' I kicked him in the groin. He staggered back, clutching himself and looking both angry and frightened. 'What are you doing?' he shouted angrily, and glared at me. He was completely offended and was struggling to contain himself.

I snapped my fingers and a pack of six wolves drew up behind me. They came round to my sides and a little in front of me, growling and slavering in anticipation as they directed their gaze upon him. Their heads stretched out in front as they looked at him pointedly, eagerly.

He panicked, looking first at them then back at me. When he saw that we were all looking at him as if *he* were under a microscope, he panicked even more. He kept trying to talk and fidgeted around. His face was white and he looked pathetic. 'Make them go away. Can't you make them go away?' he pleaded, and stepped back a little. As he did so, the growling became louder. I stepped towards him slowly and then again. The wolves stepped with me, their heads low, their teeth exposed, their eyes narrowed as they snarled at him in their fury. Uncle was walking backwards now, a look of pleading in his eyes. He then turned and walked with his back to us, turning to look every now and again. We walked after him relentlessly. The wolves were getting more restless—they wandered from left to right, agitated, impatient. I noticed that uncle had lost control and had wet himself, then he panicked completely and broke into a run.

When he got several yards away, the wolves went into a frenzy and tore after him, snarling. It was superb. They got within three or four yards of him and leaped on him. The sight of them in flight and landing on his body from above and him crumbling down to the ground was exquisite. Now they tore at him with gusto, so fast that it was all a blur. His arms and legs were kicking out helplessly one moment and then covering himself the next, trying to protect his face.

I clapped my hands sharply and the wolves immediately sprang away from him. He tried to struggle to his feet, his clothes torn. As he stood up, his face froze in terror as he fixed his eyes on me. I was changing, shrinking, and then I was down on all fours. I was one of the pack now. I growled and devoured him with my eyes. Then, in a moment of utter glee and frenzy, I tore off towards him. In only a couple of seconds I was up in the air and hit him with all my force. He collapsed. I tore at his face, his shoulder, his chest, his arm.

Blood spurted out in all directions. I was hungry. The wolves circled round leering at the bloody mess before them. I tore and I tore and I couldn't get enough quickly enough. Blood, blood, more blood. I snarled and bit and chewed and then I took his face into my jaws and penetrated his eyes. They bled. I pulled the skin off his face and he bled. He was unrecognisable and I was in ecstasy. And he bled.

He stopped moving. The others moved in and we finished off the remains.

Katy's later letter to her stepfather
It is a fine summer's day. I am eight years old. I am alone with my stepfather, John, again. I am undressed on the bed. John, the parasite, abuses me. I am frightened, confused and helpless. The parasite feeds on my fear and powerlessness and drains me.

A strange feeling suddenly comes over me. Something struggles inside, wanting to surface. I feel as though I want to be sick. It burns inside, it seethes and writhes, I cannot hold it back. Now my chest is moving, my throat hurts, I begin to choke. I can see the parasite's face through my pain. He is irritated, puzzled. I look at his stupid, drunken face. Vomit trickles from the side of my mouth. My chest is pounding—it moves outwards, the skin stretching in resistance. Suddenly my flesh tears open, splitting and bleeding. I look at his terror-stricken face with glee as blood splatters and sprays his body. My blood soaks his face, his shirt, his hands. My chest explodes and out comes my hatred, my rage in the form of a creature.

The vile, black creature rises from within my body to face the parasite. The parasite's face is fixed in terror and disbelief at the thing which he sees, the thing which his abuse has created. My creature bares its pointed, bloody teeth. Small, gleaming black eyes burn through the parasite's. My creature's large, gaping mouth is dripping blood. The parasite is fixed to the spot, unable to move, his eyes wide open in horror, his body paralysed, just as mine used to be. But now it is his turn.

My vile, bloody creature roars and pounces upon the parasite, curling itself around his face. He stumbles backwards, screaming and pulling at the creature. He falls backward on to the ground. The creature clings tightly. He screams and struggles but he is tied, just as I once was. Now he is helpless. Now he is *my* puppet. My violent, black rage tears its victim, pulling eyes from their sockets, tearing flesh—greedily, hungrily. My anger is ravenous. My creature's jaws lock into his face and rip him wide open. He is all blood. He is the victim now, just as I once was.

My rage is cold and relentless. It has no limits. I am sky-high. The creature finds that place in the parasite where I used to hurt, right in the chest, and it pulls him apart right there. Blood flies out and hits the walls. My creature eats into his heart, his lungs, his stomach, giving him the pain that I used to have. It is his now.

My creature feasts until there is no movement left, until there is no more fight left in the parasite. He is *my* victim now. A bloody mess lies inert on the floor, where the parasite once was. My creature relaxes, its hunger sated. My creature falls away and drifts. It is gone. I am one again.

Pillow-bashing

In addition to being expelled by writing, anger should also be expelled through physical exercises. Words are not always enough and can leave you in an agitated state. What can be done then? Punch a pillow. It may sound silly (and everyone feels stiff and wooden to begin with), but it is a very effective exercise.

First, kneeling beside the bed and placing a pillow in front of you, picture the aggressor's, the mother's or a problem person's face on the pillow. As in the writing exercise, the things liked about the person should first be removed and placed on an imaginary shelf, so all that is left is what the victim is angry with. With arms above the head and hands clasped together, the fists should be brought down hard on to the 'face' on the pillow. Feelings should not be held back. While hitting the pillow, the victim should say emphatically (a loud whisper will do if others are in the house) such things as, '*I hate you*!' or 'No!'

She may also use other words if she feels that they work best

for her. One client, when visualising her mother, used the word
'*Me*.' She felt it helped claim back her identity. Some victims
prefer to hit the pillow with a sports racket or similar
instrument instead of their fists. Whichever method is chosen,
the essential thing is to visualise the person the anger should
have been directed towards in the first place, so that it can be
'given' to them rather than carried around with the victim any
longer.

When doing the pillow-bashing exercise, victims should
picture themselves as the small child they once were, letting
that child express the long-repressed anger towards the
aggressor, mother or problem person. (If it is found to be
difficult visualising themselves as a child, they may find using
an old photograph helpful.) They need to let that child 'hit' the
mother, father, or aggressor with all the anger, hurt and
confusion they felt so long ago—letting that child shout 'I hate
you' and sob out the hurt that has been festering all these years.
This helps to pull the plug on the 'stop on time' and let the
pent-up emotions of the child run out freely.

Letting go of the past hurt and emotional pain is an
important step to recovery. Releasing anger from the 'child'
state will begin to free victims from depression, temper
tantrums and self-sabotage. The anger being worked on has,
however, been there since the trauma of childhood, and it will
need several goes to remove it. Writing anger letters and doing
the pillow-bashing should be done as the child they were and as
the adult they are now, expressing themselves fully from both
sides.

Other Physical Releases

Any physical exercise may be used to expel anger. Some people
who jog visualise a face under their feet as they hit the ground.
If washing windows, they can picture the problem person's face
under the vigorous rub of their cloth. One client, who has an
exercise bicycle in her lounge, pictures the problem person tied
to the back. As she 'cycles' down a bumpy, country road, the
problem person is battered along the ground. The faster she
pedals, the more he is battered. No one is hurt, and she is also
getting physically fit as she rids herself of anger.

Screaming

At times a loud scream does a lot of good. Few people have the seclusion to do this without causing alarm in the neighbourhood, but there is a way. By placing a feather-filled pillow over their face a person can scream as loudly as they want into it. If they still feel uneasy about how much sound they are actually making, it can be tested with a cassette recorder. Record the voice speaking softly, normally and loudly, then, putting the pillow over the face, scream. Usually the scream will be the same volume as speaking normally.

Some clients have found that after screaming into the pillow it felt good to strangle the pillow as well. This was particularly useful to a client who had suffered a back injury and had restricted movement.

Chairing

Another exercise for anger is one called 'chairing'. The problem person is imagined sitting in an empty chair, while the victim stands. The victim then begins to tell that person just what is felt about them, just as she did in the letters, only this time it is an oral exercise. Again, using whatever angry words feel right, the victim can stamp about the room, shake her finger at the problem person, or do whatever helps to get her feelings out.

Indirect Anger

When anger has been repressed, it can show itself as a physical illness or as fears or phobias. Since the child was never able to direct her anger towards the problem person, this anger followed the path of least resistance—inwards. Because there is no guilt involved in hating yourself, it is easier for a child to do this, rather than hating her father or mother. Often the child grows up to be a very controlled person—retreating immediately from any anger situation, afraid of expressing direct anger. Instead, she may show her anger indirectly by being emotionally damaged.

This type of anger is sometimes aimed at the whole family. It

is a subconscious way of getting even. By being an embarrass-
ment because of her emotional problems, the victim can 'hurt'
the family who let her down. The feelings of anger towards her
parents have taken such a detour that they are not even
recognised by the victim as anger and she is not aware that she
is punishing her family for not saving or loving her by having
(or being) a 'problem'. (Examples of this behaviour are
explored further in Chapter 12, under 'Getting Even'.)

It is important for a person who has repressed anger to know
it is now *all right* to be angry or to feel hate towards her mother
and father. In fact, it is essential. How can a person's hate be
exorcised if it is not first acknowledged? Acknowledging anger
is the first step to getting rid of it; denying anger is a sure way of
keeping it.

Misdirected Anger

Some victims find they have temper outbursts that are directed
at their children, possessions or themselves in an abusive,
physical way. These can be examples of misdirected anger.
Instead of tearing their children or house apart—or even
perhaps mutilating themselves—anger should be directed
where it belongs: at the aggressor and problem people from
their childhood. They need to release their anger in the
structured exercises when it is *their* choice, rather than have
anger build up and manifest itself in an uncontrolled and
inappropriate way.

One Victim's List

It is not surprising that victims of childhood sexual abuse or
childhood trauma suffer from chronic fatigue, depression or
anxiety when they have not expelled anger (or indeed any of the
backlog of feelings) towards the aggressor, their mother or any
problem people. The following is a list of symptoms associated
with her childhood experiences that *one* victim submitted to
me. Obviously, everyone will not experience *all* these symptoms,
but most victims identify with some of them.

Rachel

- Inability to concentrate for more than a few minutes.
- Daydream a lot.
- Can't keep down a job.
- Become bored quickly.
- Expect perfection from self and others.
- Over-excited and impatient when someone coming to tea.
- Angry and anxious if they are late.
- Almost constant anxiety—something eating away at me.
- Can hardly breathe for anxiety.
- Go from illness to illness.
- Panic attacks, even around friends. Fear of someone hurting me—must get away.
- Scared of getting mugged or raped by passers-by.
- Take on too much—don't know my own limitations.
- Worry sick about bills and money—can't handle it.
- Have tantrums and sulk.
- Can't wait—things have to be done *now*!
- Can't seem to get enough comfort from mate when it's given.
- I get tired of living.
- Often say, 'Nobody loves me,' but turn around and say, 'Why don't people leave me alone!'
- I use illness to get out of things I don't want to do.
- Suspicious of people's motives.
- When I get angry, I always feel guilty.
- My mind is always in a muddle—racing.
- Obsessional over trivial matters.
- Can't keep lasting relationships.
- Pessimist.
- Embarrassed about my body.
- Need a hundred and one excuses to say 'No.'
- No confidence in anything I do.
- Deny myself nice things (luxuries), but I always buy them for others.
- Can't mix love and sex.
- When sexual urges get strong, I get angry and pick a fight.
- Sometimes my mate's breathing is just like my dad's (the abuser) and it turns me on. Then I feel guilty and dirty.

Sometimes my mate even looks like my dad, even though he's not a bit like him.
- Hearing and reading about incest turns me on. I feel like a pervert.
- I get sexual feelings when I see animals having sex—I hate myself for it.
- I resent my mate having confidence.
- I don't like to see a little girl on a man's lap—I automatically think the worse.
- I say I'm sorry for nearly anything and everything—it makes me sick to be that way.
- I feel like a clown who is very unhappy yet makes everyone else laugh.

'I Don't Feel Angry'

The anger that children feel towards their parents is very frightening and threatening. That is why it is pushed inwards, away from their parents and on to themselves. Over time they perceive it to be their own feelings about themselves, and the original connection with their parents is not recognised. I have listened to clients listing enough emotional/physical/sexual abuse to generate a massive amount of anger, and yet they will sit and calmly tell me, 'No, I don't really feel any anger towards my parent(s). I just hate myself.'

If these same people heard of someone else with similar experiences, they would see all the reasons why that other person should be angry. Yet, for themselves, anger is not there. Although they may not feel anger as the adult they are now, they can be sure that the child they were did feel it. As an adult, they may have explained away the reasons for anger, but the child did not have an adult's perceptions or knowledge. The 'inner child' needs to release the anger from all those years ago, so that the adult can stop suffering its effects.

I ask clients to write a list of some (or all) of the traumatic and emotionally painful events of their childhood. I ask them to look objectively at the list. Are the things listed enough to make any child angry? If so, then it is time to start on the anger exercises, whether they are feeling anger as an adult or not. They usually surprise themselves at the extent of the anger they discover.

8   Bitterness and Self-image Exercises

Letting Go of Bitterness

There will be times—when seeing children with loving, caring parents—that victims' own barren childhood will loom painfully before their eyes. They may suddenly feel consumed with bitterness about their loss. It is not a feeling of anger but rather a calmer, deadly loathing. This is a beast they do not want to house inside for long—bitterness is very destructive to physical and emotional health.

Here is a visualisation exercise to help relieve feelings of bitterness. Sitting in a comfortable chair, relax, with eyes closed. Visualise the bitterness packed into two large bags, bulging and heavy. Struggle to carry these bags towards a fast-moving river nearby. (This is a special river, created for the sole purpose of carrying damaging emotions far away, very quickly.) Hands clenched tightly, imagine the weight of the heavy load. Then throw the heavy bags into the river. Unclench the fists as this is done, feeling how light the body seems without that heavy load. Watch the bags move quickly away, their contents dispersed far and wide. Breathe slowly and deeply, relaxing with a sense of freedom and lightness. Repeat this exercise as often as bitterness is felt.

Self-image Exercises

Most of my clients have listened to voices in their head telling them how stupid, clumsy, ugly, slow, troublesome and worthless they are—names that have become very familiar. Those are the kind of names their problem people called them as children. It is now time to turn off the 'tape-recordings' of those accusing and condemning voices. Essentially, clients are carrying those problem people around with them while listening to that rubbish in their head. When they realise that, they can see it is the same as asking the problem people to live with them!

Sentences that begin with 'You should . . .' or 'You ought . . .' are the first to go. They are not the client's thoughts—they belong to someone from their past. Accusing, condemning and negative self-talk needs to be stopped as soon as victims realise it is happening. This may take a while at first, because they are so used to listening to it. They may be in the middle of a three-day self-condemnation campaign before it finally occurs to them that they are listening to old 'tapes' of mother or whoever.

First (aloud or in their mind) they must talk back to the message on the old 'tapes', rather than meekly accepting the blaming and accusing—for example, 'I am *not* ugly [stupid, clumsy, etc.].' If the problem person's 'voice' is recognised, he or she should be called by name and told to push off and that the victim is not interested in listening any longer. Effort must be made to replace the old 'tapes' with positive input. One useful method to try is pinching the wrist upon recognising that the old 'tapes' are playing and then saying 'Stop it!' Then replace the negative self-talk with positive self-talk. Sometimes, writing down the positive self-talk will be necessary to stop the negative from starting up again.

A New Viewpoint

It is time for victims to look at themselves through positive eyes. Almost without exception, my clients have expressed feeling ugly, fat, thin, too tall, too short, etc. These are feelings that most of the population have from time to time; however, victims take these feelings to the extreme. When I suggest that they stand in front of a mirror and make a list of all their good points, I am often given a sheet of paper with just one or two attributes or with nothing at all written on it. 'How', they plead, 'can anyone say anything positive if they look like me?' This is usually spoken by people with good potential—it is not their appearance that is faulty, it is their perception of themselves.

Relearning is difficult, but not impossible. It is time to

relearn how to look at themselves and make proper evaluations. Putting themselves down is a learned behaviour, a destructive habit. Just like smoking, they have to have a desire to stop before tackling it, but it will be a lovely free feeling to be content and even pleased with their appearance. Nice to dress up and not to think that people are laughing or saying, 'Who does she think she is?' Nice to catch sight of themselves reflected in a window and think, 'She's attractive,' before discovering it is their own image.

Acceptance

No matter what my clients think they look like at the moment, they must begin to view themselves with loving eyes. One of my clients declared, 'Oh, I can look at myself like that when I get down to eight stone!' As I told her, 'Life does not begin at eight stone; life is happening right now—you need to accept yourself right now.'

All of us have known people who were physically beautiful but became ugly when they began to speak and reveal their personality. By the same token, there are people who are not physically attractive but become handsome or beautiful when their personality is revealed. Most of the people in the second category also have a tremendous smile and a ready laugh. It feels good to be in their presence. The same principle applies to everyone. Use physical potential to its limits, but let personality be the real beauty. Developing one's personality to its limits ensures a beauty far outreaching the physical potential. So, it is time to attack self-image from outside and inside.

Clients are asked to assess their body objectively, but kindly—not to get hung up on what they do not like and spend all their time moaning about it. Moaning will not change anything about anyone's body, but it will ensure that no one wants to hang around to listen to it. It takes will-power, but clients are asked to stop themselves every time they start moaning—in mid sentence if necessary. (Clients have even admitted to becoming bored when talking excessively about their ugly bits.) I suggest they try talking about the life and interests of others when the urge to moan comes on.

It is important to bathe regularly and to keep hair clean (it is surprising how many people do not) and suitably styled. I ask clients to try out some different styles of clothing and get out of any boring, unsuitable fashion ruts they may have fallen into. It is time to take an interest in clothes, hair and image—it is not vain to do so; it is what anyone who respected herself would do. After all, if people do not respect themselves enough to care about their appearance, it is not likely that other people will respect them. Inner beauty is what matters, but people have to be approachable before anyone can see if they have any. Not many of us rush out to find the inner beauty of down-and-outs.

Protection

It is important to understand that many people who suffered abuse as a child now use a scruffy, plain, threatening, thin or fat appearance as a form of protection. They feel it helps keep people away and saves the effort of trying to cope with closeness. However, once a victim starts using the exercises in this book and begins to feel some relief from guilt and shame, it is time to develop a new identity and let go of the old one. Besides, once it is looked at closely, it becomes quite apparent that the old 'protection image' never really worked—the person's life still had plenty of hurt and despair. In fact, the scruffy, plain, threatening, thin or fat appearance often invited trouble instead of warding it off.

Love Yourself

'I just want to be loved,' I wailed to a friend. 'You won't let anyone love you till you love yourself,' he replied, and suggested I start by looking in the mirror and saying 'I love me.' The words stuck in my throat, 'I love . . . , I love . . . , I love mm . . .' I couldn't do it. It took me two months to accomplish that simple task—my first step on a long walk.

I stood in front of a full-length mirror and could only say that my arms and legs were in working order and all my bits were in the right place. All my bits were in the wrong proportion as far as I was concerned, but I did not say that aloud—I was making my first attempt to speak positively about myself. I complimented myself on my hair texture, eye colour, ear shape and feet. Not exactly the items to qualify me for a beauty contest, but they did qualify me for the first step to a better self-image. As in any learning process, it was two steps forward and one step back. I tried not to be too concerned when I had a really bad day and hated the sound of my own name, let alone the rest of me.

I often put the following question to my clients, in order to make the point of accepting their appearance: 'If you fell in love with someone, would you toss him aside because his body was not perfect?' The answer is invariably, 'Of course not.' Perfect bodies are obviously not the most important factor in choosing a partner, or else 99% of couples would not be together. If clients feel they can love someone who has skin problems, weight problems or a big nose, or is bald, bow-legged, etc., I ask them, 'Then why don't you think someone could love you with whatever "flaws" you label yourself with?'

They must keep in mind the fact that their self-image was damaged by the problem people in their childhood. They must not let problem people win this battle and so be robbed of their opportunity to like themselves. They have been robbed of too much already—it is time to throw off the rubbish these problem people have loaded them down with. Change will not magically happen: clients must stand tall on their own legs and claim what was taken—their self-esteem. It must be nurtured and treasured like the valuable commodity it is and not be belittled or rejected by calling it 'vanity' or 'conceit'.

I ask clients to make a pact with themselves that every time they say something negative about themselves it must be counteracted with something positive. Because they are not used to saying nice things about themselves, that becomes very difficult to do. (The difficulty, in itself, can be a deterrent to making the negative comments in the first place—'Oh no, now I've got to think of something good to say!') Again, I encourage clients to be creative and to think up other exercises to encourage a positive outlook. Whatever is done, they must stop comparing their face and body to the media image of 'young and beautiful'. The make-up, photography techniques and touch-ups are what create 'young and beautiful'— those male and female models look fairly ordinary at home in their jeans and dandruff.

The Mask

Jade has written about a very common experience among victims—the feeling of living behind a mask:

Jade
Hello, my name is Jade. I'm the girl behind the mask. Well, I'm not a girl, I'm a child. The mask is grown-up, but I'm not. You see I'm too afraid to take the mask away, afraid of what people will see. It's like being badly disfigured and not wanting to reveal yourself to people.

But I am disfigured—not physically, but emotionally. Let me explain. As a child I was abused, rejected and hurt. I was left feeling guilty and ashamed and my whole world was lying around my feet in thousands of pieces. I had nothing to cling to, no one to run to, and to me it was my fault. I have been crying ever since, and that is where the mask comes in.

The mask is doing two things. Firstly, it is making me look normal and grown-up, which is the physical reason. Secondly, it is *helping* me to grow up, giving me information and help. (Because the mask is 'adult,' whereas I am 'child'.) The mask of adulthood can make me see that the abuse wasn't my fault: it is a tissue for my tears, a cuddle for my insecurity and a reason to grow up.

I have a very special friend (my therapist) who also used to wear a mask, but not any more. When we see each other, my mask comes off and for that short while I am the one *behind* the mask. My friend helps me to sort out my thoughts, helps me to realise that I haven't done anything wrong. It is hard work, because you have to face yourself, believe in yourself and like yourself. Remember what I said about being disfigured physically? It is the same feeling being disfigured emotionally, because, if you have always hated yourself, imagine what it is like to reveal that to someone else.

I hope you can understand a little bit about the girl behind the mask. I am going to work my hardest to throw it away. Sometimes that thought can shake you, but you can't hide behind your shadow forever. One day this little girl is going to grow up and give and receive all the love she never had. No more guilt, no more shame, no more rejection. I am picking up the pieces very, very slowly and when it is all put back together and all the cracks have been smoothed out, the mask will disappear—for ever!

Jade's mask (the pretence of adulthood) was useful to help her get through life and to hide the humiliating fact that she really considered herself to be a child. While talking to her therapist, she could admit to and expose her 'child' safely and learn how to help the 'child' feel secure. Her goal is to actually become an adult, when she will be able to throw the mask (the *pretence* of being adult) away. So, the mask is both helpful (keeping her 'child' protected) and a hindrance (making her feel a phoney).

Image of Contamination

Katy drew the following picture to show what she used to see when she looked in the mirror. Katy, the grown woman, saw the dirty, ruined and contaminated child she believed she was. Because this image was what filled her eyes, she believed that others saw her 'contamination' too. As a consequence, her behaviour began to follow the same belief and she developed social phobias, unable to mix her 'contaminated' self with others whom she saw as 'clean and whole', not 'ruined'.

Damaged Image Turns to Damaged Behaviour

Rachel has written about the effects that abuse had on her life and how she felt after she started therapy. As she says, the work is hard, but not as hard as living with the damage done by the abuse.

Rachel

I was seven years old when my dad abused me. He forced his penis into my mouth and I had to swallow the ejaculation.

At that time I had two brothers and one sister, all younger than me. By the time I was ten there were two more, one sister and one brother. We were a middle-class family. My dad was American and we travelled back and forth from America to England every few years.

Mum and dad argued quite a bit. My mum tended to be

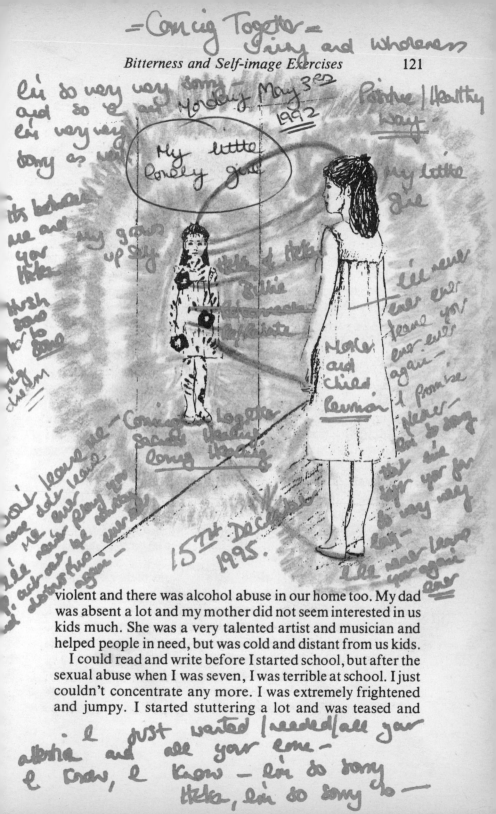

violent and there was alcohol abuse in our home too. My dad was absent a lot and my mother did not seem interested in us kids much. She was a very talented artist and musician and helped people in need, but was cold and distant from us kids.

I could read and write before I started school, but after the sexual abuse when I was seven, I was terrible at school. I just couldn't concentrate any more. I was extremely frightened and jumpy. I started stuttering a lot and was teased and taunted by the kids at school. I used to cling to people who showed me any attention. I hung on them like a leech practically, until they would finally push me away. It was a pattern that stayed with me into my adult life. I don't remember any cuddles from my mum, I can't remember her cuddling any of us kids. I just avoided my father as much as possible. Once when we were still quite young, my sister, five years my junior, told me my dad was interfering with her. In later years, however, she denied anything had ever happened.

During my teens I was very depressed and suicidal. I never caught up at school. I still couldn't concentrate and still stuttered very badly. I needed affection so much I began to trade sex for those few moments of the only kind of intimacy I was familiar with. Sex became a complusion for me, I couldn't get it off my mind. I never stayed with one boy for very long. I wanted them to like me but when they did I couldn't like them anymore. I guess it was *me* I hated so much and I couldn't think much of anyone who would like such a terrible person as me. Even though I had all that sex, I never really enjoyed it, not like you are supposed to. I mean it was never really satisfying, in any way. During those years, I used to get anxiety attacks and would stay up all night cleaning the house. I just couldn't sleep. I never trusted anyone. It seemed my only communication with people was the sexual thing.

I left school at fifteen and lived at my parents' home with my boy-friend, in my bedroom. He was violent and abusive and very possessive. I became pregnant and we moved into our own place a few months before my son was born. I was sixteen then. During this time my father left my mother and went back to America.

My marriage ended after two years and plenty of abusive behaviour from my husband. I lived rough with my son and was drinking heavily and taking drugs. I couldn't find work or a place to live. Finally I was unable to cope any longer and gave my son to social services. I just drifted after that. It all became a blur of bad times, drink and drugs. At the end of two years I ended up in a mental hospital. They let me out after four months and I made a suicide attempt, so they took me back for another two months.

I met my present husband a short time after I was released from the hospital. We were married, and a year later I was able to get my son back from the social services. For the next eleven years I was very unstable—never balanced. I had violent mood swings. Slowly I alienated myself from everyone around me with my tirades, violence, manipulation, suspicions and general unpleasant behaviour. I had developed physical ailments: colitis, stomach ulcers, allergies. I was agoraphobic. I felt guilty and unable to have fun or relax. I felt so guilty about relaxing I hardly let myself rest. My violent behaviour become worse and I felt I needed to go to the hospital again.

In February of 1987 I read a newspaper article about Penny Parks and the work she was doing with victims of incest. My husband rang her for me, because I was still stuttering very badly, and we made an appointment to go see her. I was surprised to see a woman who had confidence and vitality, because her childhood experience was much worse than mine. For the first time I began to wonder if I too could be normal at last.

My husband sat in on the counselling sessions at first, which I requested because I was unable to retain information very well. Penny gave me a load of pamphlets to read and a couple of exercises to do. Some of the exercises were OK and others sounded really silly, but I promised to do as she suggested.

The parenting and pillow-bashing exercises were the hardest for me. I was reluctant to find my 'little girl' and give her comfort, maybe because I had always thought of her as the 'bad' part of me. I had been busy running from the 'little girl' and here I was being asked not only to face her but to embrace her! The pillow-bashing was difficult to get started with—I'd keep putting it off for later. Once I was able to let out some of my anger (and there was a lot of it) I did get more violent towards my husband and son for a while, so I had to learn to focus my anger into the exercise, and not out of it. I learned to go bash a pillow when dealing with certain kinds of anger. I still use it as a coping skill, but as an adult rather than my 'child'.

All of the exercises were hard work, and I had to force

myself to do them at times, but slowly they became easier. I began to see changes in my feelings and actions. I faithfully read all the books Penny suggested and found them really helpful in understanding some of my behaviour. I particularly liked the books about transactional analysis and assertiveness. It helps knowing that growth is accomplished by 'two steps forward and one step back', because I don't feel so devastated now when the 'one step back' happens. It's hard work, but the way I was living before was much harder.

9 Growing Up

Childish Behaviour

Victims often find themselves, as adults, displaying childish behaviour. For instance, they may be very fearful of putting petrol in their car at the petrol station, worrying that they may do it wrong and make a fool of themselves. When angry about something, perhaps they throw a childish tantrum. Others may have problems during conversations, by butting-in in an attempt to direct the attention to themselves or by trying to 'top' other people's stories with 'Yes, but listen to what happened to me . . .' or 'You think that's bad—I . . .'

If people find themselves just waiting for the other person to end a sentence so they can begin again, maybe it is time to examine their motives. Have they really something that crucial to say, or is it only a reluctance to let go of the warm feeling of attention one experiences while speaking? If that is the case, it may be that the 'child' is operating where the 'adult' should be.

'I CAN'T'

Take notice of how many 'I can't' statements are a part of the everyday vocabulary? 'I can't' because of fear, lack of confidence, lack of money, lack of opportunity, etc. In many cases, the actual words are 'I won't.' (Obviously, being on the dole, say, makes it impossible to buy an expensive car or to fill the house with new furniture, but it may not prohibit getting out and travelling by bus, walking or getting a lift with a friend. It may not prohibit making one's home interesting and attractive with inexpensive or second-hand items. It is more productive to make the most of what you have than it is to do nothing and build up the role of being one of life's victims.) Challenge the 'I can't' statements and see if they are covering up an 'I won't' statement.

Is the 'child' sitting, dejected, lonely and feeling sorry for herself, watching the others play, watching life pass by while moaning 'I can't do that because . . . ?' It is up to the adult to comfort, support and teach the 'child'.

When childish behaviour is recognised, it can be controlled. Take the chance and walk up to that petrol pump—ask someone for directions if unsure. Anger can be dealt with consistently to avoid a tantrum building up. If a tantrum does occur, it is important to apologise instead of justifying it. It is also time to try to avoid butting-in. Listen to the other person for a change—concentrate on having a whole conversation without talking about 'me'. By giving some warm feelings of attention to someone else, one can learn to enjoy the art of giving. Then, when others do ask something personal, it will be the warmth of genuine attention that is felt, rather than the hollow and unsatisfying result of forced attention. We can call that experience 'learning the art of receiving'.

Victims can either set their minds to learning and trying or sit and let the ghost of their childhood say 'I won't.' There are no knights on white horses to rescue anyone—we must all rescue ourselves.

'It's Their Fault'

Clients often tell me that if their family, friends or partner would start to treat them better then their own behaviour would improve. Wrong. First, this is asking everyone around them to change—even with mass hypnosis, this is unlikely to happen. Second, if everyone else did change, the victim's behaviour would be reinforced—there would be no need to conduct herself as an adult.

People will treat others with respect when their actions deserve it. To receive respect and love, it must be given. If victims are dominating every conversation by interrupting, that is what they will get back from the other participants. If they sit mutely waiting for others to draw them out or to be struck magically with the art of conversation, they will get back what was put in—nothing.

Approval

One of the biggest breakthroughs for me was being free of my mother. She did not die, go away or stop speaking to me—in fact, our relationship went on as usual, but with one crucial change—I did not need her *approval* any longer.

For years the uncomforted child within me had been wanting, needing and trying to get my mother's approval. The harder I tried, the less I received from her. I would then rebel and do things I knew she did not approve of, but I always came back to trying to win her attention again.

Mother took up a fundamentalist religion; I took it up too. Mother was very active in the church; I was more active. I thought she would look at all the good works I did and feel proud of me; instead, she seemed resentful. If my grades at school were As and Bs, she would criticise, saying she did not value educated people much because common sense was what was needed in life. To me it seemed that whatever happened in my life, mother was not there for me, was not on my side. I felt that if I did something good, mother criticised it; if I had problems, then mother said 'I told you so.' I felt damned if I did, damned if I didn't.

Suddenly I realised that my mother was the same person she had always been. Because of her background, lack of education and the generation she was brought up in, she lacked many parenting skills. Nothing had changed since my childhood— she still lacked these skills. I could see I was expecting behaviour from her that she was incapable of, and maybe even incapable of understanding. As long as I kept waiting for her to relate to me as I wanted, I would be bitterly disappointed. It was like expecting an untrained horse to run a race—she was just as unprepared, emotionally.

I became aware of all the ways in which I had 'set up' tests for her and, when she failed them, thought to myself, 'See! She doesn't care about me or she wouldn't . . .' (My greatest underlying fear was that she really did not love me or—worse —that I was unlovable.) I do not know why I had thought that she was suddenly going to break a lifetime's behaviour pattern to show me some love or support just because I had arranged an opportunity to do so.

She often said she had given up so much for me and suffered so much for me and I did not appreciate it. As an adult, I could see that that statement was not entirely true. She had boxed herself into corners for reasons to do with fear, immaturity and lack of knowledge. In reality, she often sacrificed, rejected and blamed me. She had manipulated facts to be able to see herself as a totally self-sacrificing mother. That may have been what she wanted to be, but it was not what she was—nor is anyone. When she failed, it was easier to blame me than to admit to herself that she was wrong or had made a mistake. I also recognised that from her example I had learned the same behaviour: that it was not permissible to make mistakes and, if you did, you should try to blame someone else.

However, none of what she did or did not do had anything to do with me, or with lack of love, on her part, for me. She did not know how to cope with life or children very well. She did not know how to save herself, let alone anyone else. Her emotional needs were so strong and unmet that she could not deal with anyone else's. It was like asking someone who is starving to give the crust of bread they have just found to some other starving person—few people have the strength to do that.

Changing Oneself

I could finally see it was up to me to view my mother as she was, not how I wanted her to be. I had to face the fact that she would possibly never be what I wanted her to be, that she would probably continue to let me down. The only thing I could change was me. Seeing mother as she was did not mean that I was filling my image of her with negative attributes but rather that I was viewing her realistically—perhaps for the first time learning to give her permission to make mistakes, to be the human being she was.

Facing mistakes from the past can sometimes take more courage than the average person has. It is easier to drift along. If I had lived my mother's life experiences (which were very traumatic) with her social and academic education, in her generation, could I say that I would have turned out better? I could really only describe what I hope I would have done.

I had also to realise that whatever my mother decided to do, or not do, was up to her and had no bearing on me getting back my emotional footing. It was as though I had been trying to get her unconditional approval before I would approve of myself, before I would allow myself to grow up. That could involve a long wait. Maybe, I thought, I had better take responsibility for myself and get right to work on this business before I lost too much more time.

To myself I said, 'OK, from now on I am not going to expect anything positive from my mother. If something positive happens, that will be nice, but I shall not look for it. I will stop looking for her negative reactions too—stop stacking up black marks against her. If something negative happens, I will not be surprised and I will not be accusing. I would not be angry or give a lecture on manners to a small baby spitting its food on its chin. Perhaps my mother is no more capable of positive parenting than the baby is of keeping its chin clean.' After all, I was certainly having a pretty difficult time learning positive parenting skills for myself, and I was *trying* to do so. It was unlikely that those skills were going to just drop out of the sky on to my mother, so why should I be expecting them to?

It began to occur to me that perhaps my mother was doing the best she could and had too much on her plate to deal with successfully already. Funny—I had always thought she was 'OK' and it was just me who was unable to cope and 'not OK'. It stood to reason that, if she had too much to deal with in the first place, parenthood was going to be the straw that broke the camel's back. Positive parenting was going to be the last thing she could do.

I continued with my personal affirmation: 'I shall rely on myself and my partner/friends/associates for my positive input and emotional support. I shall avoid subjects I know will cause a disagreement with my mother and stick to superficial conversation, if need be, to keep from being drawn into a negative exchange. I will remember that my mother has not been, cannot be, and probably never will be "there" for me emotionally—I shall stop expecting it.'

I counsel clients to look around at their family, friends and acquaintances to evaluate which of them provide emotional support. I suggest that they should surround themselves with the people who give them positive support, as often as possible.

Very often they have friends with a negative attitude about life in general. Continually listening to negativity would be defeating the purpose of trying to recover one's self-worth.

Cut the Cord

Having decided on the pattern of future relations with my mother, was I an 'adult' at last? I felt like it. A great weight had lifted off my shoulders and I began to get on with my life. I had cut the cord between my mother and myself. It seemed funny, then, that I had taken so long to do it. It was as if the 'little girl' inside me had waited in the hope that someone would come for her. She thought it was going to be her mother. It turned out to be me—the adult.

Slowly, I became the mother/woman I had always wanted my mother to be. Using the exercises to get rid of anger, guilt and bitterness; making the decision to stop expecting something unattainable from mother; and using the exercises to 'parent' the child within me had given me a freedom I never thought possible. My self-confidence grew. My awareness of what I wanted to be grew. Of course, like any learning process, it was two steps forward and one step back, but I finally understood that process and was not unduly upset by it.

Being 'Ready'

One thing I noticed when I started teaching my methods to others was this: no one could absorb the information unless ready to face the past. So, clients who were brought to me by someone who wanted help *for* them often either were not able to absorb the information given them or were unable to make a commitment to do the work. They usually went away with nothing more than the knowledge that I was there whenever they decided they were ready. It is sad to see people walk away when you know your information can help them, but it would be sadder to try to force something on them they were not ready for and end up convincing them that they were unable to be helped.

On the other hand, when clients would seek me out for help of their own volition, remarkable progress was generally made.

Some clients were able to regain their emotional footing in as little as a few months; others might take a couple of years. (The average recovery time is six months to one year. Working without a therapist will lengthen the time.)

The type or duration of the abuse makes no difference to how fast a person sorts herself out. Someone abused for years could recover within a year, and someone else with minimal abuse over a short period might take a couple of years to come to terms with it. So, one experience of abuse could be just as damaging as years of abuse would be. The abuse itself, as frightening and confusing as it is, is not as crippling as the effect of the betrayal the child feels at the hands of trusted adults. When trust—that vital link with the adult world—is severed, fear and misplaced guilt are turned inward, creating emotional isolation. The resulting warped self-image and perception of life are what leave the child emotionally mutilated. Therefore, the extent of injury varies with each child.

10 Communicating with Parents and Children

Parents

Conquering the need to gain my mother's approval, as described in Chapter 9, and making good progress with the 'parenting' exercises had given my 'adult' a lot of self-confidence. In fact, I now felt I had enough to spare, so I thought it might be a good time to try to improve communications with my mother. I began by trying a few experiments with her.

My mother had never been able to cuddle or hug very warmly—usually quick, firm squeezes was all she gave. I decided to try to teach her a new way to hug, by example. So when I hugged her next, I did not let go quickly, as she did. She was confused and responded by giving me another quick hug, then another. I finally had mercy on her and ended the first lesson. In the following weeks, she slowly began to see that I was not going to stop hugging until I was ready. She also (what choice did she have?) began to hug me back in the same manner—no more quick hugs. Even better, she enjoyed it.

After the first few times, I added a bit of verbal input—nothing elaborate, just positive and personal. 'You've made the Christmas tree look so beautiful again.' 'What a lovely colour dress you're wearing.' 'I like your hair that way, Mum.' 'Those flowers make a nice homely touch to the house.' Or I might just say, 'I love you, Mum.' She seemed to blossom under these new attentions. She too hugged spontaneously and made positive statements. I could actually feel a warmth from her. I still had no expectations of her—she could just as easily start on a tirade of criticism as before—but when the displays of warmth happened they were welcomed and encouraged.

Keep in mind, however, that the old 'childish' ways may

surface with angry thoughts such as, 'Why should I have to make all the first moves? Why do I have to risk myself? *She's* the mother—*she* should show *me* the right kind of love!' If this happens, have a gentle word with the 'child' inside and ask her to just relax and let you, the adult, handle the situation. Then carry on with the behaviour chosen for use, rather than blindly giving in to behaviour that belongs to the 'child'. If the 'child' anger thoughts are very strong, an informative and comforting letter about the situation should be written to her.

Before my self-parenting experience, mother would lecture me on what she thought I should and should not do. We would have long arguments, when I would defend my point of view and she would impose and interrupt with hers. Time for another experiment, I decided. Obviously we were not going to change each other's opinion by arguing, so it was time for plan B. When mother presented her opinion, I said, 'I understand how you feel, but I have different views. I think we should talk about something else.' Of course, she at first kept on talking. I would then repeat, almost word for word, my statement again, and again and again. Either she would get fed up with my repetition (like a broken record) and shut up, or I might have to say, 'I'm sorry, Mum, I don't want to discuss this any further. I'm leaving for now. See you later.' Then I would leave. She soon got the message that I would not be drawn into a discussion just to argue. All the time, I kept my voice calm but firm.

The 'broken record' method, which I had learned from an assertiveness course, did wonders for me and how I felt during visits to my mother, and she seemed to respect me more. One thing which must be mentioned at this point is that if people expect their mother not to tell them what to do, then they must, in return, respect her rights. It does not matter how she treats their brothers, sisters, aunts or uncles. They must forget about her politics, religion, racism or sexism and keep their opinion to themselves about her clothes, hairstyles or make-up. Unless there is something positive to say about those things, it is time to keep quiet—just as they want mother to do for them.

This is all part of cutting the cord—of behaving like an adult with parents. Much of the interaction with families is learned behaviour. It is time to relearn something that frees victims to be their adult selves. In a few cases people find their families so inadequate that they stop seeing them altogether, while others simply limit the visiting time. However, they may discover that their new behaviour *improves* the relationship.

Face to-face Confrontations

To regain emotional health, it is not necessary to have a face-to-face confrontation with the aggressor or with the passive parent. In fact, I discourage this unless a client feels very strongly that she wants it. In that instance, I prepare my client to get through it with as little damage as possible—prepared to face possible denial and rejection, sometimes from the entire family.

Almost without exception, an aggressor will deny the charges and call the victim a liar and a troublemaker. Whole families can side with the aggressor, because it is very threatening to face that incest could be a problem in 'our family'. This is extremely traumatic for victims, who are left feeling even more unloved and isolated than before. They thought justice was going to be done at last, and are now shattered. Most victims' families offer very little assistance on the road to recovery. Fortunately, however, the family's help is not necessary for the victim to become whole again. Families do not even need to know about the efforts being made to regain emotional health. This is something victims can do for themselves, leaving the family to sort out their own problems.

Generally, my clients end up writing off the aggressor, even if he is their father. They often do not feel a need to try to mend or salvage the relationship. In these cases, the aggressor is viewed as 'just a nut case', not worth bothering about', 'a pathetic person', 'a wasted life', 'too far gone', or 'nothing to do with me anymore'. Some may tolerate the aggressor's presence at family get-togethers for the sake of the others, but do not want to interact with him.

Other victims make it clear to the rest of the family what the aggressor has done, and will not attend family gatherings if he is invited too. A few aggressors actually go into therapy and learn new, healthy ways of relating to others, and in doing so are able to resolve the past. In that case, family relationships can sometimes be salvaged and warmth and understanding be attained that were never there before. When a client wants to try to have a proper relationship with the aggressor, it is usually necessary that family counselling specifically designed for sexual-abuse cases be used to mend the damaged relationship.

Can Aggressors Change?

One problem is that aggressors do *not* change unless they are treated by the proper professionals. These must be professionals who are especially trained to counsel incest aggressors. (Gracewell Clinic, a treatment centre for abusers, can provide advice and help. See the list of Helping Agencies at the end of the book for details.) No matter how insistent they are about their remorse, or how pathetic they may appear, aggressors will soon be caught in the same situation again if they do not get professional help. Aggressors who are finally admitting what they have done can be very convincing about how sorry they are and swear it will never happen again. 'I just didn't know how it was affecting the child. I'd rather cut "it" off now than hurt a child again.' Rash statements like this are commonplace, but unless professional treatment is obtained, the abuse *will* all happen again.

It is a fact that aggressors never get too old to interfere with children. Grandfathers and stepgrandfathers have often been named as aggressors by my clients. Even when they may be too old to have regular intercourse, they can still use their hands and mouth on children, and force the children to do the same to them. The same goes for abusers who are taking medication that renders them impotent (medication for high blood pressure etc.)—they may not be able to have an erection, but they can do plenty with hands and mouth.

Prison sentences keep the aggressor off the street and away from children, but what happens when he comes out? He will resume his old activities, unless the proper professional help is available. Realistically speaking, it is impossible to purge every child-molester of his desires. Much could be done for him, but there are additional measures to take to help protect children.

Communication with Children

First, the subject of sexual abuse of children must be faced openly and honestly. It must be taken out of the realms of taboo to be sure that everyone knows and understands it. Children should be trained by their parents to be aware that they can say 'No' to unwanted touch—from anyone. Parents should back their children up when they show reluctance to kiss a relative, perhaps letting them shake hands instead.. Children need to know that their bodies are their own. They need to know that they have a right to say 'No' to kisses or touches that feel uncomfortable or that they do not feel like having at the time. Children who are pressured into unwanted physical contact will be more vulnerable to a molester—they will have learned that they have no choice and that their feelings of discomfort do not count. Children need to be encouraged to trust their inner feelings of what seems right or wrong, instead of having them overridden by parental commands. Otherwise, children will associate parental approval with unwanted kissing and touching from adults. That association leaves the door wide open for children to believe an abuser who says, 'Mummy won't like it if you don't kiss me, if you don't be nice to me.'

When past abuse has not been sorted out, victims also feel trapped into co-operating when they encounter similar abusive situations as an adult. The ability to say 'No' therefore applies to adults as well—particularly to women victims who are facing sexual harassment. It is important for them to learn to trust and respect their own feelings. If a man makes a pass or an inappropriate comment, women need to know how to say 'No'. They do not need to give a reason or an explanation—they can simply say, 'I don't feel comfortable about that.' If pressed further, they can calmly ask, 'Why are you questioning me?' and walk away.

Lines of communication must be kept open with children about sexual matters. If someone interferes with them, children will then feel able to ask for help. On the other hand, if children know that a rude word, a question about where babies come from or 'playing with themselves' is met with shock, anger and punishment, who are they going to be able to tell if someone interferes with them? They will simply assume they cannot tell anyone, because mother will be even more shocked and angry with them than she was before.

One little ten-year-old girl was interfered with by her grandfather in a house where an aunt was at the time. The child told her mother later, and was asked if she had thought of calling for help from auntie. The child replied, 'Oh no, Aunt Ruth gets very upset if you even say "fart". I knew I could never tell her about this!' Parents need to be more realistic and open about sexual subjects with children. Puritan attitudes that block communication can cause children a great deal of suffering.

'It's a Secret'

Many parents, discovering their two- or three-year-old playing with himself, over-react and slap the child's hands, saying angrily 'That's *very* naughty. Don't ever let me see you do that again.' End of explanation. Children of that age are not masturbating with the same motive as an adult. It is just a pleasant feeling—perhaps something to do when bored (which is probably why they seem to do it at times that are most embarrassing to their parents—for example, when sitting bored on a church pew, in a supermarket trolley or during a visit from mother-in-law).

It is a good opportunity to use the situation as a teaching experience. Children will never be stopped from having a fiddle in their trousers, but it can be redirected. 'I know that feels nice to do, Timothy, but it's not polite. It's rather like picking your nose—that's not polite to do, is it?' (The child can relate to this kind of comparison.) 'So, you should do that when you are on your own—maybe in your room. OK?' Using this method can help children change their behaviour to be socially acceptable. It does not condemn children, nor block any future communication about their private parts. Just telling children, 'Don't do that!' has never stopped them playing with themselves, so why continue giving a useless command?

An angry outburst does not explain *why* parents are upset. Children just know that mother was cross when they touched their private parts. They will only conclude that they must not talk about that part of the body to mum. If a child-molester comes into the picture, that is where he will touch the child, and that is why the child will believe him when he says, 'You will be in trouble if you tell.'

Children do forget, so, when little Timmy is entertaining himself in an inappropriate place again, just remove his hand gently and say firmly, 'No, darling, it's not polite to do that here, remember?' Perhaps you can offer him a distraction: 'Tell mummy whenever you see a red tin on the shelf' (if you are shopping), or 'Tell mummy about the kitty you saw next door.' If possible, offer a toy or a book to give him something to do. Just do not make a performance out of an innocent child's action. If we want children to be able to tell us about abuse, we must keep the lines of communication open about their bodies.

The same rule goes for whenever children ask questions that parents were not expecting. 'Mummy, what does "fuck" mean?' 'It's a rude word that is used for the word "mating".' 'What's mating?' 'It's when a male plants a seed in a female.' For a small child, that is generally enough information to answer the question. It is senseless to punish or shout at children because they have repeated a rude word. If children ask questions that parents cannot think of an appropriate way to answer, the parents can stall for time. 'That's a very interesting question. Let me think about it and we'll talk about it later.' Be *sure* that it *is* discussed later. Also, plan ahead—think what answer might be appropriate to certain sexual questions that are likely to be asked.

Children can provide a wealth of amusement in their innocence—enjoy that aspect of them too. My six-year-old daughter proclaimed, 'Mummy, I know the daddy plants the seed in the mummy and the baby grows in her tummy, but how does he plant the seed? Does he use a shovel?'

Parents cannot keep ignoring areas that make them feel uncomfortable or in which they are ill-informed. If parents are unsure of what to say to children about sexual matters, it is time to look for some books on the subject. Parenting responsibilities in this area must be taken more seriously.

It's a Secret

It's a secret,
Daddy says.
No one should know
Except me and him.
It's our special game.

Be nice to your new daddy,
Mummy says.
Mind him,
Do what he tells you.

Daddy, I don't like our game,
It hurts me, I'm afraid.
No, I don't want to go to jail . . .
Mummy will too believe me!

I told.
Mummy's mad at me.
She says I'm a liar.
Daddy says I'm lucky,
I could have gone to jail.

Oh well, I'll just keep pretending
I'm somewhere else.
Maybe daddy will get tired
Of his game.
I hope mummy won't be mad any more.
I promise I won't tell again.

                                             Penny Parks

11 Sexual Dysfunction

People who have been sexually abused as children must now look at the situation realistically, not through the eyes and understanding of a child. Realistically, an adult chose to sexually infere with a child—to cause that child to become aware that her sexuality existed before that would naturally happen to her. That does not make her sexuality bad, dirty or wrong; it only makes that adult wrong. Nothing children say, do or think can *make* adults do anything they do not *want* to do.

Male victims

Boys who are victims of sexual abuse have usually been abused by a male, and this can cause them to question their sexual identity. If they then leave home at an early age and find it difficult to get work, it is not unusual for them to go into prostitution. Gay Search's *The Last Taboo* (Penguin, 1988) quotes statistics showing that almost all male prostitutes (and 75–80% of female prostitutes) have been victims of childhood sexual abuse.

Few girls are stimulated to orgasm by abusers, whereas boys are more often stimulated that far. They then feel betrayed by their own bodies, questioning their sexuality. 'If I'm feeling pleasure from a man, I must be homosexual.' They are then burdened with two secrets. Some never divulge the information to anyone and carry a great weight of guilt, based on childhood perceptions and misinformation, for the rest of their lives. Some may even become child-molesters as adults. Certainly their relationships with women can be fraught with sexual and emotional problems—adding to their confusion—and can possibly push them towards turning to children to satisfy their emotional and sexual needs.

Even when a boy tries to find information to help him with his sexuality, there is not much available that relates to incest victims. Nothing to tell him that if his own thoughts and fantasies revolve around girls, then he is heterosexual. Or that even an interest in boys and/or sexual contact with his peers is a normal experience in adolescence and does not necessarily mean that he is homosexual. Being interfered with by a man does not automatically change a boy's sexual preference. Equivalent principles apply to girls' sexuality too.

A boy who is attracted to his own sex may think that the abuse happened *because* of those feelings. He may think that the aggressor could 'see' what he was feeling, and so fears that everyone can 'tell' what he is feeling inside. Sexual abuse does not verify homosexuality, and the aggressor would abuse whether or not he perceived a sexual preference. Nothing the child has done, said or thought has provoked the adult to sexual abuse—provocation came from within the adult himself. In fact, the abuser does not take the victim's needs/preferences/ feelings into consideration at all—those feelings are irrelevant to the abuser.

Children may clutch at the idea that it was somehow their fault, as that gives them a feeling of control. Accepting that the adults had total control means that children must accept the fact that they are powerless. That can be too threatening to face. Putting blame on to themselves, although it presents a whole host of problems, at least seems to give some firm ground too. For, if they believe that they somehow made it happen, then they believe they must also have the ability to stop it happening again.

That reasoning may seem vague and flimsy to an adult, but to children, desperate for stability, it makes sense. Of course, when they cannot stop the abuse from happening, the circle of guilt and shame continues.

FEMALE ABUSERS

When boys are sexually abused by a woman, they may develop into impotent or sexually restricted adults. The damage caused by the sexual abuse is far greater if the abusing woman is the victim's mother, for children perceive the nurturing, protecting role of their mother to be even greater than that of their father. Children who are abused by their father can still retain the fantasy that their mother is all right, even if she is distant and they cannot disclose the abuse. Abusing mothers not only deprive their children of a nurturing/protective relationship but also leave them bereft of hope for one. In a child's eyes, theirs is the ultimate betrayal.

LOVER SUBSTITUTES

In my own practice, the males who came to see me about emotional abuse showed a very interesting pattern of behaviour problems when their mother had 'smothered' them with inappropriate closeness—that is, as a 'partner'.

Mothers who treat their sons as a lover substitute *without* sexual activity can cause serious damage as well as those mothers who are using sexual activity. A mother may make her son 'head of house' (with or without the father in the home) and encourage the son to pass judgement on her clothes, hairstyles, etc. before she makes her decisions. Although never overtly sexual, the relationship is of an intimate nature. Inappropriate jealousies often surface when girl-friends come into the picture during the boy's puberty.

Loyalty to the relationship that the mother created is difficult to disengage from, especially when the mother is around during adult life to pour on the guilt. Since the relationship was never defined by actions or words, the young man feels guilt from what he thinks was there, and guilt for thinking something was wrong if somehow the mother was innocent.

For these boys, sexual subjects may be treated as disgusting by the mother, as well as normal bodily functions or nudity. As the young man reaches puberty, he feels more guilt from his natural interest in sex, girls, masturbation, wet dreams and fantasy. These taboo subjects sometimes stir some undefined sexual feelings that he also recognises as having been in his mother's relationship with him. He probably blames himself for these feelings, not understanding the role his mother has played, and is left feeling bad and dirty.

As a result, for some of these men, sexual relief in adulthood will sometimes be ritualised, or involve people they normally would not be in contact with, such as prostitutes. In that way, a victim can separate himself from the act to a degree. If he is able to participate in a relationship with a person he knows and cares about, sometimes the sexual side will have to follow the distancing pattern he has devised to deal with his sexuality. These patterns may include sexual games, dressing up or dressing his partner up (usually as a tart or a stripper), being tied up or being dominated. (These last two both remove responsibility.) Sometimes intercourse cannot or can seldom be accomplished, and mutual or separate masturbation is substituted. This may have to be accompanied with certain props, such as special fabrics or fur, pornographic books or videos, or costumes. All the things just mentioned can be part of any healthy sexual relationship—they become cause for concern only if one or more of them is a ritual and the *only* way to any sexual gratification.

Female Victims

Among those who were abused in childhood there are women who cannot be penetrated, women who cannot have an orgasm, women who are not interested in sex at all, and women who are not interested in men at all. On the other hand, there are also women who have a great deal of sex without physical satisfaction, women who have orgasms but cannot form a loving relationship, and women who think they must have sex with every person they go out with in an effort to feel loved and important.

There is the common problem of associating sexual feelings with the experience of the abuse. 'If I feel turned on, I'm no better than *he* was.' 'If I get close to someone in a relationship, will he be able to tell what has happened to me?' 'I like to cuddle and kiss—it's the other part I hate.'

Females also question their sexual orientation. Many feel repulsion for men and for the act of intercourse, even if it was not fully accomplished during the abuse. Some are repelled by the vulnerability they feel with males. Those women may direct their sexual desires towards women. Some transfer all of their emotional and sexual needs to women; others may have a heterosexual relationship but use their fantasies of women to cope with the sexual demands made by their partner. As a woman begins to understand and cope with the events of her childhood, and regain her emotional health, she will be able to view her own sexuality free of childhood perceptions. The important thing is not whether people are homosexuals or lesbians but that their sexual orientation is a natural one, not something dictated by childhood trauma.

To have sexual feelings is normal. Having sexual feelings does not connect the victim to the abuser, does not make her 'like him'. The abuser ate food too. Would the fact that the victim eats food make her 'like him'? Desiring sex is just as normal as desiring food. Victims must not let abusers rob them of their sexuality. They must not readily turn their back on it but, instead, be willing to embrace it, protect it and wear it proudly. Sexuality is one of the more beautiful gifts life has. It is time to start reading about it, appreciating it and enjoying it wisely.

Information to the 'Child'

As victims begin to learn about their sexuality and how it should be operating, they can share this new information with their 'child'. They should write letters to their 'child', explaining how the incorrect beliefs originated, what the correct attitude is and how to adopt it. Below is a letter from Anne to her 'child' giving this information.

Anne

Dear Anne

You spent a great deal of time when you were little trying to be a 'good girl' because you believed that if you were good your parents would really love you.

When the time came for you to begin to become sexually aware of yourself and others, it happened that you were held up to your classmates as an example of 'badness'. This was not true and not fair, but you were badly hurt and harmed by it. It reinforced your need to be seen and accepted and loved as 'pure' and 'good'. To achieve this you needed to deny yourself a normal interest in sex and, in consequence, your sexual development has suffered. You have many inhibiting beliefs and you must change these now.

You grew up believing sex was 'naughty', 'not nice' and 'bad'. But sex is good. It really is. It is not just for having children. You have areas in your body designed especially to experience sexual pleasure. It is good to feel pleasure. Allow yourself to relax and enjoy the sensations of being touched. If you feel and express this pleasure you will give pleasure to your partner also, and this shared pleasure is very good.

You grew up believing that, if you allowed the real 'you' to show, you would be rejected. You would become vulnerable and exposed and that vulnerability would be ridiculed just as it was when you revealed something of yourself when you were twelve years old. This is wrong, because what happened then will never happen again. You are an adult now with an adult's strength and understanding. You will not be revealing yourself to a mob of immature children but to an adult and loving husband. So relax and don't tense up. Allow yourself to become excited—it is OK. Let go of your thoughts—don't cling to your mind with its analysis and control, just abandon yourself to desire and pleasure. You *are* lovable in this state too, you know. The ability to abandon yourself to desire and to pleasure is part of being whole. Self-control, detachment and coolness are fine and necessary qualities in many circumstances, but not in bed! You need also the freedom to be passionate, wanton, lustful and hot, to be a complete person.

You grew up believing that your body was unattractive and that only the beautiful could enjoy sex. Don't feel so self-conscious now. You do have a nice body—you're not fat and you are not unattractive—so enjoy it. Your perfectionism really lets you down here. You run yourself down because you don't look like a movie star or a fashion model—but who else do you know who does? You do *not* need a perfect body to have good sex. You just need to be responsive to an appreciative partner. So enjoy your body for what it is—really good enough for good sex.

When you were young you did not explore or experiment with sex, but it is never too late to learn and you are ideally placed now to start. You have a patient and loving husband and a desire within yourself for completeness. Things have never seemed so promising. Reach out for the happiness and wholeness that is there.

Fantasies

While reading a book on women's sexual fantasies, I discovered that fantasies about children being molested sexually excited me. I was shocked. My first thought was, 'Oh no, I'm going to be a molester!' Yet, since I had no sexual interest in children, I decided not to panic but to take a little time to work it out.

The first sexual stimulation experienced makes a definite impression on people. When a similar situation occurs or is read about, there is a mild form of stimulation surrounding the memory. It does not matter if the memory was good or bad; it just registers as an experience that is familiar. When experiencing the situation in fantasy or by reading something similar, there is an accompanying feeling of being in control. The victim is the one saying what happens next: *she* is powerful; *she* is in charge. She is not in the role of a vulnerable, helpless, terrified and confused child. Instead she is in charge, even if, in the fantasy, she is representing the child.

Small children often use play time to re-enact traumatic events. Putting such events into her play gives a child the same sense of control. It is simply a coping skill to deal with fear and confusion. It is not an unusual experience, and it does not mean there is anything 'bad' about the person. It is merely a way of sorting out some feelings about a confusing situation.

On the other hand, if victims are being sexually aroused by children directly, it is advisable to contact a professional service for help. (See the list of Helping Agencies at the end of the book.) Remember, the feelings will not go away on their. own, no matter how good the intentions.

Changing Attitudes about Sex

What happens if victims are sexually dysfunctional (impaired) in some way? What can be done about it? Rather than accepting the attitude that sex (or aspects of it) is disgusting, it is time to look at sexuality as an important possession that has been stolen. If a person had been forced into a wheelchair from childhood, although nothing was wrong with her legs, she would not be able to walk. Her leg muscles would need to be built up and exercised before she could use them. The same thing has happened to victims' sexuality. There was nothing wrong with it originally, but they were forced to view it as useless to them because of the circumstances of their childhood. They must now view it as being as valuable as their legs, and put as much work into learning to use it as they would their legs.

Unfortunately, we are living in a society that is afraid of sexuality and shies away from discussing it. Victims would get all sorts of help if they actually had a problem with their legs, but they will have to work harder to get help with problems concerning their sexuality. They are certainly not the only people with sexual problems—all those people who are afraid to talk about 'it' have problems too. One certainly does not have to be a victim of sexual abuse to be sexually dysfunctional. Victims are lucky in one way, for at least they know the direct cause of their problems and therefore where to start to solve them.

It is important for victims to look at the aggressor in their life and to realise that this person has robbed them of the free expression of their sexuality. Then they must learn what they were prevented from learning before.

Learning about Sex

Victims can buy or borrow whatever books about sexuality they find suitable. If they have problems with pictures, start with a book that has more words. *Questions of Sex* by The Diagram Group (refer to the Book List for details of this book and others) is an excellent small book to help clarify the confusing information that most victims have about sex. I find that most of my clients have very little sexual knowledge and information. Most are badly misinformed because they have never been able to face the subject of sex. They were never free to ask questions, so they had to be content with whatever they overheard. Even reading about sex would embarrass them to the extent that they could not absorb much of what they had read. Also, some felt that to know about sexual things would make them somehow guilty and dirty. I have spent a great deal of time answering a wide variety of questions for clients about sexual matters, hoping to impart not only information but also a relaxed and healthy attitude towards sex.

As an adult, I was able to have intercourse and able to have orgasms, but not at the same time. Orgasms only happened when I was manually or orally stimulated. I did not know that a large percentage of women are the same, because it is often difficult to achieve the right contact between your clitoris and your partner's pelvic bone. Some people's bodies fit together in a way that makes orgasm easy for the female; others do not. I had felt defective that I could not reach orgasm during intercourse; I was happy to learn that I was basically normal. At that time in my life, I was unable to discuss anything about my sexual needs with my partner, nor he with me. I just hoped something magical would happen to make sex better. Waiting for magic or a new partner on a white horse to rescue me was useless. It was more useful for me to learn about my own sexuality and how to communicate with my partner about sexual matters. My sexual problems were up to me to solve.

DEVELOPING ONE'S SEXUALITY

Read and learn how the body can respond sexually. There must be an active attempt to accept sexuality as a good and natural thing—which it is! If one has a loving, supportive partner, it will be an easier job. If one has a closed, uncooperative or even abusive partner, there will be a difficult time ahead—not impossible, but difficult. If one has no partner at all, it will be a bit of a one-sided effort, but there are ways to learn in spite of that.

Most people feel comfortable with cuddles, so start with them. (If victims do not feel comfortable with cuddles, they should work through their sexuality problems with a therapist, rather than tackle them alone.) If possible, the partner should be told about the abuse background and asked for understanding and patience. (If that is not done, he may be a bit confused and feel rejected.) Victims should start where they feel comfortable and then add one more step that they can *just* tolerate, until that becomes easy. Each time they gain one step, another should be attempted. For instance, a woman might feel happy to cuddle but freeze up when her partner begins to touch her more intimately. She should start with a step that is giving her an active part, not just lie back, switch off, and hope things will magically change. (It also helps to start where one feels a little more in control, rather than passively accepting whatever comes next.) She should perhaps try kissing her partner's neck, and see what kind of response she gets. If her partner is enjoying that attention, she might begin to nuzzle his ear, nibbling and kissing. (Be careful not to deafen him with loud, kissing noises!)

As she becomes happy with that—which may take a few weeks, months or sessions—she may move her attention a little lower. A man's nipples are very sensitive, and many men enjoy the same kissing, licking and sucking action that a woman can enjoy. She may gently stroke her partner's body—and, no, that does not mean just his genitals. She may stroke his hair, face, arms, hands, neck, chest, back and bottom—not necessarily all in the same session, but just as she feels comfortable. She can make it an opportunity to show love and caring to her partner. Just holding his hand to her face and kissing it, enjoying the feel, texture and fragrance, can be a pleasant experience for both of them.

She can use whatever books she has chosen to read about sexuality and think of steps that can be added to her repertoire. The idea is not to be able to utilise 101 positions but to at least learn what is available and how to enjoy what appeals to her. The biggest favour she can do herself is to keep reminding herself that it is *all right* to enjoy sex and to give pleasure as well. Then she should make an effort to relax and let her partner touch her—remembering that it is OK to enjoy it, that that is what her body was designed to do! There may be touching she can tolerate and touching she cannot. Again, she should start where she feels most comfortable and slowly condition herself to enjoy her sexuality.

WHAT IF THERE IS NO PARTNER TO PRACTISE ON?
If she is without a partner, the woman has more of a challenge, but there are things she can do. First, she must follow the steps of teaching herself what sexual responses can be and educating herself to know her own body. Once she has done both of these,

she can begin to condition her thinking. In a quiet, undisturbed place, she can use fantasy/visualisation to explore the techniques described for use with a partner. In fact, some clients use this method before they try it with their partner.

She should imagine a partner as clearly as she is able to and slowly familiarise herself with the thoughts and associated feelings of being touched, kissed and looked at. (It may take some practice to get used to this type of exercise.)

Picturing one experience at a time, she should continue with it until she feels fairly comfortable. Then she should move on to the next step, just as she would do with a partner. Slowly, she will absorb positive pictures and feelings about interacting with a partner. Enjoying sex is mostly an exercise of the mind, so she will not be that far behind her friends who have a partner, for each person must give themselves permission to enjoy their sexuality.

Penetration Problems

If the woman has problems with penetration, she must start by getting to know her own body. On her own, with no worry of interruption, she can use a hand mirror to examine her genitals. She may first want to familiarise herself with what all the parts are called and look like. That information is easily available at the local library in any book on anatomy. She should choose the one that looks the easiest to understand and take it home to study. When she has her mirror in place, she may have a look and see what she can identify. The clitoris is the bit that brings her to an orgasm.

It may take a few sessions to get relaxed with this exercise. It should not be overdone, just taken slowly, five minutes at a time if necessary. She should keep in mind that it is only her body, not an evil force to be wary of. It is each individual's responsibility to know their own body and care for it.

When she feels comfortable viewing herself, she can then insert one, then two and then three (clean) fingers. She will see how easily the opening accommodates three fingers. Using one finger, she can feel the walls of the vagina, the different textures and shapes, feeling as far back as she can, becoming familiar with herself and at ease with her body.

Some sex-therapists give varying sizes of dilators (sometimes glass or rubber, penis-shaped) to their female patients who find difficulty in being penetrated. The patient starts with the smallest and progressively adjusts to the largest. Whether dilators or fingers are used, the important thing is actively to attempt to change the negative attitude towards one's body.

Internal Examinations

A woman can use the same method to prepare herself for internal examinations by the doctor. Most of my clients found internal examinations difficult—some impossible. Some women feel more comfortable with a female doctor. The doctor should be told about the childhood abuse background. There is no need to go into a long, detailed story—a simple 'Doctor, I was a victim of sexual abuse as a child, so I have difficulty with internal examinations' will be sufficient.

Past Experiences

Many victims have had their first experience of oral sex in their childhood, as well as experience in masturbating a man to ejaculation. For some, these memories are too difficult to overcome completely. If that is so, do not worry about it. There are numerous sexual acts and positions, and even people who have not been abused do not use them all. If some sexual activities are infused with unpleasant associations that cannot be overcome, do not worry—they are not essential to enjoying a fulfilling sex life. If a former victim finds one or two positions satisfactory, that is sufficient. There is no need to feel pressured to use more. Quality is more important than quantity.

Discussing the Past

When former victims start to heal and become more relaxed and adjusted to their background, they feel happy to discuss it when necessary. They do not feel panic, shame or fear. They look at themselves as someone who was merely an innocent victim, with no blame or guilt on their shoulders. The more they regain their emotional health, the more happy and eager they become to share information with other people who are still captives of their past or people who are interested in learning about childhood sexual abuse.

When discussing the past, my clients have found that people respond to them best when the information is shared in a relaxed and confident manner. In this way they help put the listener at ease. There are exceptions, of course, and it may be found that people who are the most uncomfortable are sometimes those with sexual problems themselves, or perhaps they have had an association with sexual abuse and are not yet ready to face the subject. Whatever the case, it is *their* problem. It is best to allow them the right to be uneasy, change the subject, and carry on feeling confident and relaxed. After all, if it takes victims a while to absorb the information of childhood sexual abuse and feel comfortable with it, why wouldn't other people have a similar problem?

Seeing a Professional

When seeking help, use every avenue open: sex-therapy clinics, counselling, psychotherapy, support groups, books, etc. But if a counsellor, a group or a book is placing blame or responsibility on to the victim, rather than on to the abuser, it is wise to end that association—it simply means that the counsellor, the group or the author of the book does not have proper information about the subject of abuse and will not be very helpful to victims trying to recover from the past. After all, if Freud, the father of psychoanalysis, could be so wrong as to believe that incest victims had fantasised their abuse, some modern-day counterparts may have incorrect information as well.

Victims should *never* believe any counsellor or therapist who tells them that their problems will be solved by having sex with them. The counsellor/professional should not touch the client's body in an intimate way (or have the client touch the counsellor's) as a form of therapy either. If a counsellor/professional needs to explain how different intimate parts of the body work, a plastic model or a picture can be used. Equally, a counsellor also does not need to touch a client's genitals to 'make sure they are in working order'—a common ploy used. (Obviously there are examinations, of an intimate nature, for legitimate therapeutic or medical reasons, but you should expect these to be carried out in the presence of a nurse or a female assistant. However, there is no legitimate therapeutic or medical reason for a client to have sex with a counsellor or any other professional.)

There have been some unfortunate cases of women being exploited by men in the helping services. Those men need help themselves. Women should say '*No*' and leave immediately. There are charlatans in every vocation, but that in itself should not be considered a reason to avoid getting help. No one would leave their car unrepaired because some mechanic quoted them a ridiculously high estimate—they would simply find another mechanic with better prices. If a woman has been approached by a charlatan counsellor or other professional, she should simply find another with better professional manners. She might also consider reporting the unprofessional conduct to whatever body governs that particular field.

12   Blocks to Recovery

'Poor Thing'

There are a few things that can stop personal growth. First is the 'poor thing' image. Some people are so used to being a victim that it becomes their only identity. In their opinion, everything *always* goes wrong for them, and they are *always* hard done by. Family, friends and acquaintances *always* let them down, and no one treats them with respect. The partners they want seldom want them, and they tend to end up with someone who treats them badly and eventually leaves them.

Their lives have been full of self-sabotage. Their conversation is full of 'I can't do that' statements. Their posture is usually stooped and their head slightly down so that they are looking up at people most of the time—a cowering body stance. These people view themselves as 'poor things'.

By being 'helpless', they feel that people will rush to their rescue. They react as small children who are dependent on adults, but operating from the emotional standpoint of a small child does not work for an adult. People do not rush to the rescue. In fact, most people become annoyed and try to force the 'poor things' to help themselves.

The idea that their own behaviour is causing most of their unsatisfactory relationships never occurs to the 'poor things'. They may be convinced that someday someone will come along to rescue and be good to them, protecting them from unkind people who are short-tempered and demanding.

I have also found that 'helpless' people are very good at finding people who, for one reason or another, have a *need* to 'help' people. These people with a need to help are very often victims themselves. They see helping behaviour as a way to feel useful and to be accepted. In the end, it is a cycle of a victim abusing another victim.

When these 'helpless' people come forward for therapy, they run into a few problems. At first, they have a willing audience to talk to about the abuse and consequent troubles in life. The therapist understands their feelings and problems. So far, so good. But when real commitment to therapy is required, the reply is consistently 'Yes, but I can't . . . ,' followed by reasons why it will not work for them.

The idea of giving up the helpless 'poor thing' image is too frightening. How would they ever relate to anyone? How would they get anything they need? Who would have a reason to like them if it was not for their needy state? These are some of the questions in the back of their minds while they make 'Yes, but . . .' excuses.

The fact that this role has not actually gained anything for them thus far is overlooked. 'Poor thing' feels comfortable to them, like an old friend. To abandon it would feel like being stripped naked in front of everyone.

I try and give these clients an overall view of their behaviour pattern, of the negative effect it can produce for them. Giving comparisons and information about other 'poor things' who have changed their image can also be helpful. The parenting exercises are particularly useful to these people, because it is the child within them that is constantly reaching out for affection and attention. When they themselves can give those responses to their child within, the need for others to fill that role diminishes.

However, any decision for change must come from the client. Most choose to try the new—even though fearful— paths, but some cannot leave the imagined security of the old ways of the 'poor thing'. They may be ready at a later date to try for a change, or they may just continue telling everyone how they were sexually abused as a child and how terrible it all is. They are living out their life as a victim.

Getting Even

Another hindrance to growth can be the need to punish parents. Victims may feel that if emotional health is regained then there is nothing they can use to indirectly punish mum or dad. Many victims discover, after going into therapy, that they had secretly enjoyed their parents' distress about the emotional problems they (the victims) had, because it was a way of getting their own back. This was not a conscious thought, but a controlling one. Even people who have not experienced sexual abuse may employ the same type of retaliation over hurts and disappointments from their childhood, but no one can get better while solely bent upon punishing their parents.

These people tend to feel that, no matter what method they try, they will never regain their emotional health. It may work for everyone else, but not for them. In a way they are right—it will not work for them, because they will not let it. Some people attend class after class, see counsellor after counsellor and read book after book, all to little avail. They are not suffering from lack of information, but they will only allow themselves to apply it to a certain degree—just enough to hover on the brink of health and then fall back into the pit, or, more precisely, step back into the pit. Whatever phobia, illness, or behaviour pattern they have chosen may be aired and shaken out from time to time, but the 'hiding cloak' will be clutched tightly around them again if emotional health gets too close.

(Note: the term 'hiding cloak' refers to any behaviour that victims hide behind so that they can avoid facing the real issue. For example, if suffering from a food/drug/alcohol disorder, illness or phobia, they can spend all their energy dealing with that and never have to face the issue of sexual abuse and the crippling fear (although untrue) that in some way it was all their fault, that they deserved it.)

Sometimes clients can break through this with the parenting exercises. I may give anything from subtle suggestions to outright statements outlining their particular 'hiding cloak', but, again, until clients are ready to look and accept, change will be slow in coming.

Another method used to help victims to recognise their problem is to get them to draw up two lists—one headed 'Advantages of Being Emotionally Healthy' and the other 'Advantages of Being Emotionally Unhealthy'. Often what comes out in the lists is a surprise to victims. After looking at the following lists, the young woman who wrote them said that she thought the 'Healthy' list would be the longer. She could hardly believe she had written the entire 'Unhealthy' list. It was an insight into herself that was very useful. It would be a pity to sacrifice one's entire life for the sake of getting even.

Katy
[By 'her', Katy is referring to her mother in these lists.]

Advantages of Being Emotionally Healthy

1. Independence from her.
2. Pride, self-respect.
3. Freedom.
4. Be separate person from her.
5. So I can be different from her and like myself better.
6. So that I don't identify with her and feel inferior to others—i.e. feel 'normal'.

Advantages of Being Emotionally Unhealthy

1. Reminding her. ('See what you've done.' 'It's your fault.' 'I'm like this because of you—that's how bad *you* are.')
2. Cry for help. ('Do something about this—you're to blame, you solve it.')
3. Trap her, she has to face it.
4. Make her stop ignoring me. She has always pretended I'm OK, never taken me seriously. Problems have been shoved under the carpet very quickly, not even acknowledged. I'm forcing her to *see* my problem. (Every time she thinks of me, she must think of me in that context. She can't push me out altogether because of love. It's unbearable for her to see me *with a problem*—but no choice!)
5. (a) If she faces my problem, she'll be forced to look at her own and she'll get better. She'll change. Then I can respect her more. Then I'll be better motivated to recover, myself.
   (b) If she gets better, then she'll get strong. If she's strong, I'll have something harder to kick against. Then I will calm down and be more accepting, be tamer. I can be less controlled because if the other person is in control I can let go and feel freer. While she's weak, I have to

be over-controlled because if I lash out she can't take it. Urges (aggression, etc.) have to be repressed *tightly*. (Same with friends.)

6. Being a millstone round her neck is our only link. If I stop that, there will be nothing. We'll be very separate, two different people, like strangers. No relationship. If I stop it, she'll be let off, which is what she wants. I want to weigh her down. To disappoint her, remind her.

7. Showing her who's mother. *Her.* I'm not going to be the strong one. She wants me to mother her. This is unacceptable (anger, contempt). *She's* got to mother me. I've got to be *more* vulnerable than she is, to show her her role.

8. To prove she's a bad mother. Punish her.

Being Overwhelmed

Looking at a host of problems and attitudes to overcome and relearn can be quite daunting. Victims may feel like throwing their hands up in despair. It is hard work, but so is the effort involved in masking emotions.

I like to compare sorting out emotions to sorting out an overcrowded hall cupboard. When the door is open, all sorts of rubbish, treasures and forgotten items fall out on to the floor. What a mess! It is tempting to shove it all back in and force the door shut. But, no—having decided to tackle this cupboard, sleeves are rolled up and work begins. It is started by separating things into three piles: 'Keep', 'Throw away' and 'Undecided'.

Soon the person is surrounded by a larger mess than at the beginning. Usually, at this stage, their partner, mother, children or friend comes in and says, 'Can't you do that some other time? What a mess! This is inconvenient for *me*!' Some frail souls may give up at this point; heartier ones say, 'Sorry, I must sort this out *now*.'

People will find forgotten things (emotions and behaviours) in their cupboards and others they do not know what to do with. These must be dealt with one thing at a time. Sort them out first, into the three piles. Some behaviours, like those belonging to 'poor thing', will go in the 'Throw away' pile. Even though the behaviour seems comfortable, it is destructive to relationships. Like an old jumper, it is out of style, shapeless, and full of holes. You may, at the last minute, weaken and want to retrieve the old jumper (behaviour) before its final journey to the dustbin, but that impulse must be rejected—excess emotional baggage is not needed.

Slowly sort through the 'Undecided' pile. Examine each item to see whether it is a personal opinion or the opinion of others that one has picked up over the years. Opinions are like habits—people often develop them without thinking. For instance, it was my opinion that worrying and fretting for family members, when they were late coming home, was showing love for them. I would pace the floor and imagine road accidents, car trouble and all manner of mayhem. When they returned unharmed, I would then shout at them for 'worrying' me, and we would usually have a row. Of course, my parting line would be, 'I wouldn't worry about you if I didn't love you.' (This is probably one of those statements passed on from generation to generation.) This was one of my opinions, turned emotions, turned behaviour that was in my 'Undecided' pile.

To change this habit, I first asked myself how useful 'worrying' was. When nothing bad had actually happened to my loved ones, I still ended up shouting because I was worked up to such a state. If something actually *had* happened to them, my emotional energies would have been depleted through working myself into a state and I would have been ill-equipped to cope with a serious problem. So, I learned to tell myself, 'You don't *know* that anything bad has happened, so carry on as though it hasn't.' I kept myself busy and distracted and pushed aside any 'worry' thoughts that tried to sneak in. When my loved ones returned, I could then be prepared to greet them with a big hug and a kiss and say, 'I'm so pleased to see you!' They now *felt* loved and I felt like a loving person.

As I examined my life, I found several areas of this kind where I wasted my emotional energies (and did my physical person some damage at the same time). I learned to put my emotional energies to work *for* me. These behaviours changed from 'Undecided' to 'Throw away.'

If victims are 'poor things', 'getting even' or feeling 'overwhelmed' by their problems, they can still take heart. Yes, the work is hard, but the reward will be the most precious treasure possessed. It is the freedom to be themselves. When they have finished sorting, they will feel proud of a job well done, showing off their tidy 'cupboard' to close friends. No more reason to steer people away from it, warning 'Whatever you do, don't open that door!'

11ᵗʰ April '92   ✳ 0836 ✳

I have got to open my inner doors to say fuck it, yes it all happened really to me Helen Stafford but I am not going to let it eat me destroy me for one day longer, I will not be a victim one day longer, I will not become twisted and bitter, otherwise I am just the same as them. I must I will reclaim my life my self

I will risk all and step out into the light / life. It has all kept be buried, hidden for 36 years no more. The old Self has to go completely forever   crucified forever, let go

13 Questions and Answers

The following questions were submitted by clients.

Q: Is it possible for an incest victim to recover completely?
A: Yes, but the length of time it takes depends upon each individual. By recovery, I do not mean forgetting the past but rather ending the pain of the memories and so preventing life from being overshadowed further by the past.

Q: Does recovery depend upon confronting the aggressor in person?
A: No. I do not even encourage this. Victims need confront no one but themselves to regain emotional well-being.

Q: Is counselling necessary for an incest victim?
A: Certainly discussing it, even with one other person, is useful. Some people can sort themselves out without counselling, but when good counselling is available, it is wise to take it.

Q: What would happen if a victim did not seek help at all?
A: A small proportion of victims are able to work out their problem without help. For the remainder, it will continue to be anything from a bothersome problem to a crippling handicap. Problems are not wished away—victims must seek help and then apply it, whether it comes from a book such as this or from a therapist.

Q: How can an incest victim help herself?
A: By reading and learning about childhood sexual abuse. By following the suggestions and exercises in this book. By joining a support group. By seeing a therapist.

Q: What is the most important thing to do in order to recover?

A: Victims must stop blaming themselves for a crime they cannot in any way be guilty of.

Q: What is the most crippling effect of incest?
A: Self-sabotage, caused by misplaced feelings of guilt.

Q: What are the signs of incest in a child (who is suffering at the time) and in an adult (who suffered in the past and has not yet been helped)?
A: In a child, school difficulties (inability to concentrate), bed-wetting and soiling, nightmares, troubled sleep, suddenly needing a night-light, lots of new fears, returning to younger more babyish behaviour, not wanting to be left alone, suddenly turning against one parent or relative or a friend of the family, loss of appetite or a sudden increase in appetite, unusual behaviour shifts (from gregarious to withdrawn, or easy-going to fearful), clinging, needing more reassurance, sexual knowledge beyond the child's years, expressing affection in inappropriate ways (such as French kissing), a sudden change in play habits, fear of schoolyard, church or neighbour's house.

A few of these signals may be present in any child, whereas children suffering sexual abuse show *most* of them. If these signals are evident, parents should enquire gently about the child's feelings. *Keeping Safe*, by Michele Elliott, and *No More Secrets*, by Caren Adams and Jennifer Fay, are two excellent books to help parents talk to children about their fears. (See the Book List for details.)

The most common signals in adults are self-sabotage, nightmares, phobias, sexual dysfunction, insomnia, agoraphobia, obesity or anorexia, low self-esteem, immaturity, aggressive or withdrawn behaviour, poor self-image and lack of confidence, alcohol or drug abuse, and panic attacks. (Although low self-esteem, poor self-image and lack of confidence may sound like the same problem, they are different in the following ways. 'Low self-esteem' refers to people who feel that they are worthless—ruined and soiled. 'Poor self-image' refers to people who believe that they appear repulsive to others or believe that they do not deserve to look attractive and make efforts not to. 'Lack of confidence' is a feeling that you will never succeed and so efforts to do so are not made.)

Q: Is it necessary to recovery for adult victims to inform their mother about the abuse if it happened in the past?
A: No, recovery does not depend upon confronting the mother. However, in order to protect other children from the aggressor, it may be necessary to bring the past to light. Each case must be judged individually.

Q: Can telling one's mother about the past *help*?
A: Sometimes it explains past behaviour of the victim and answers some questions the mother may have had. In that case a closer bond can be established. It can also help other past or present victims to come forward (brothers, sisters, cousins, etc.). Victims should, however, be aware that telling their mother can also cause them to be rejected and disbelieved. Many families would rather not know, would rather not be burdened with guilt, are not ready to face something they may have been trying to forget or find too appalling to accept. Just because victims are ready to face their past does not mean that everyone else in the family is ready as well. So victims must be prepared—they may meet some uncomfortable reactions. I do not suggest confronting family members with information about abuse until the victim is fully recovered and able to cope with possible rejection. To do so before recovery suggests that the victim is simply indulging in self-sabotage behaviour.

Q: How can knowing about the past affect a victim's mother?
A: Some mothers are shocked and hurt, but supportive and helpful. Other mothers are overwhelmed by anger and guilt and react defensively or accusingly. They may deny the abuse or blame the victim. This behaviour is not a reflection of feelings about the victim, but rather the mother's own feelings of guilt and failure.

Q: How early can you begin to teach a child how to prevent or deal with an abusive situation?
A: As early as one would begin to teach traffic safety, fire safety or safety from other dangers to children.

Q: What are the main rules to teach children about preventing sexual abuse?

A: Teach children they have a right to say 'No' to any unwanted touch. Teach children that sometimes even nice people or people we know may do something that confuses or frightens us. Teach children always to tell (and keep telling till someone believes them) when they are confused or frightened by something happening to them. *Then* back up children's rights to say 'No.' For instance, do not insist they give grandma or Uncle Charlie a goodbye kiss when they show a reluctance to do so. Suggest a hand-shake instead.

Q: Will early sex education protect a child from sexual abuse?
A: No. Children will only gain some measure of protection from sexual abuse by knowing how to say 'No' to unwanted touch, how to avoid being bullied and how to recognise a bribe. Sex education of itself does not provide this information.

Q: What sexual problems can arise in adult life for an incest victim?
A: A wide variety of sexual dysfunction, ranging from an inability to be cuddled to an inability to be penetrated. Misplaced guilt is at the root of most sexual dysfunction. Sex is associated with the abuse, and therefore pleasure connected with sexual activity in adult life may be viewed as bad or in some way linking the victim with the aggressor. If pleasure does break through this emotional barrier, the victim can experience remorse demonstrated by tears or verbal abuse of their partner in an attempt to nullify the pleasure. It may also be unbearable for a victim to participate in some sexual acts first performed with the aggressor. Victims interfered with by an abuser of the same sex usually question their sexual identity.

Q: How does the aggressor justify what he is doing to the child and how can he continue to do it?
A: First of all, many aggressors do not see what they are doing as harmful, or hold the view that children forget as they grow up. Others are trapped within their own personal inadequacies and cannot comprehend anyone's pain but their own. When an aggressor does try to justify his actions, he may adopt the same viewpoint that most people use for explaining

other socially unacceptable relationships: 'It's different with me.' Frequently the blame is shifted to the child or to the mother. Reasons that may sound flimsy to begin with seem to gain strength when repeated to one's self numerous times. Some aggressors have the opinion that they own their family and can do what they choose with it. Whatever the web of justification an aggressor weaves, it serves to keep him buffered from the reality of what is happening.

Q: If the mother secretly knows that the child is being abused, how does she manage without taking action?
A: Denial is the coping device most widely used. Sexual abuse in one's family is a devastating fact to face. If a mother has inadequate coping skills, she will not suddenly be able to become strong and face things squarely. Once something has been denied, it becomes easier to continue to deny it. A pattern is set.

Q: Why does a mother disbelieve her child when told of sexual abuse?
A: Her child's abuse experience may be similar to experiences from her own past that she cannot face because she still feels misplaced guilt. Therefore she may deny it. The social stigma attached may be too much to bear, or she may worry about the family falling apart emotionally and financially. It is easier to deny and call the child a liar.

Q: How does being called a liar affect the child?
A: The child feels betrayed, abandoned and angry. It is often too threatening to display those feelings to her mother, so they are directed inward. The child blames and hates herself.

Q: Is it possible that the aggressor loves his child, even though he has abused her?
A: Yes. Loving someone and having the maturity to behave responsibly towards her are two different things.

Q: If an incest victim is able to enjoy sex in later life, doesn't this mean she enjoyed the abuse?
A: Not at all. If there were pleasurable feelings during the

abuse, it only means that the child's genitals were working properly. If, as an adult, sexual activity is pleasurable, it means the same thing. The two acts have no connection.

Q: Is it possible that an adolescent might claim to have been abused as revenge against an adult?
A: It is possible, but unlikely. Children know adults are not willing to believe them, so they would be putting themselves in a very vulnerable and exposed position. Sexual abuse is a difficult allegation to prove (even with penetration). Without a confession from the adult, the adolescent knows it could all fall back in her face. Few adolescents would take that kind of risk to get back at someone.

Q: Is family counselling able to resolve the problem of sexual abuse?
A: Properly trained sexual-abuse counsellors working with the whole family have shown the best results in repairing the damage and breaking the repetitive cycle of abuse.

Q: Is there a typical home setting in which abuse happens?
A: The class, financial status, race or religion of the families vary greatly. But some of the common denominators of the parents' emotional make-up are child-like emotional needs, inadequate coping skills, low impulse control or over-control, poor communication skills, authoritarian attitudes, sexual abuse in either or both parents' background and a tendency to invert the parental role by drawing on the child to meet their own adult emotional needs.

Q: If an adult has blocked childhood abuse from memory, what causes the memory to return?
A: Sometimes a particular emotional trauma or series of stressful events, or perhaps another case of sexual abuse in the family coming to light. At other times the memory may surface if the person is undergoing therapy. Any time when emotional energies that have been used to keep the abuse hidden have to be used to cope with some other crisis, the memory can surface.

Q: If a child experiences physical arousal during abuse, does

that make the child partly responsible or a weak person?
A: No. The responsibility belongs entirely to the abuser—the child is merely a vulnerable person who has been victimised. Physical arousal only means that the child's genitals are working properly.

Q: Without any knowledge of sexual behaviour, is it possible for a small child to seduce her father?
A: No. With or without sexual knowledge, it is not possible. Children are loving beings who offer their devotion whole-heartedly and innocently. It is the adult who introduces sex into the relationship. It is the adult who is responsible for setting safe limits. It is the adult who has control over the child. A child cannot make an adult do things that the adult does not wish to.

Q: If a child tolerates abuse because it is her only source of affection and physical contact, doesn't that make the child partly responsible?
A: No. It is the parents' responsibility to give the child proper love and attention so that she is not compelled to settle for anything else.

Q: Why don't children protest more or tell more often?
A: Children are easily intimidated and frightened into silence by an adult, and even more so when that adult is their own parent. Furthermore, children think it is somehow their own fault and are afraid to tell.

Q: Do aggressors have addictive personalities?
A: Some do, but it is not a common trait for aggressors to use drugs or alcohol.

Q: If the aggressor is especially intelligent, does this make him more dangerous to the child?
A: It may mean he uses more sophisticated forms of emotional blackmail, but he does not have to be intelligent to trick and manipulate a child. I would not say it makes him more dangerous than a less intelligent aggressor. The damage to the child has to do with trust *being* broken rather than with how it is broken.

Q: If a victim has blocked the abuse from memory, can it still affect her?

A: Yes, the same emotional problems will be evident, but a skilled therapist can help a client work through her emotional problems even if the exact cause is not known.

Q: Is it likely that the sons of victims will become child-molesters?

A: Not unless the son becomes a victim himself; then the likelihood is increased.

Q: Are the children of female victims likely to become victims?

A: There is a risk of this happening, because of the tendency for some former victims to marry abusers.

Q: If a victim's past comes to light, will she be offered friendship just because people pity her?

A: No more than if there had been a death in the close family. A show of sympathy over a painful experience should be accepted as just that. There is a greater risk of the victim getting stuck in a 'victim' role, using it as an identity, becoming a 'poor thing' in her *own* eyes rather than in the eyes of others.

Q: Can incest victims ever lead normal lives?

A: Yes. Even experiences like incest can be overcome and, in doing so, a person can attain greater emotional strength.

Q: Do the relationships of incest victims flounder because of their horrible childhood?

A: This is a common problem. When our past is not coped with, it affects our present and, consequently, our future.

Q: Can victims ever feel comfortable during an internal examination?

A: Discomfort with this is a common complaint with victims, and some go to great lengths to avoid having such examinations. As women begin to come to terms with their past and learn to be comfortable with their own bodies, the fear of internal examinations diminishes. I encourage clients to tell their doctor that they were victims of sexual abuse during their childhood and so have problems with the examination. No more information than that need be given. Some women may need to be referred to a female doctor.

Q: Can a victim ever trust her father (the abuser) again?
A: Unless he has undergone therapy, he is still a potential abuser and therefore he cannot be trusted. Few post-incestuous relationships are able to be mended if the abuser does not receive help.

Q: Can victims overcome their sexual dysfunction?
A: Yes. When victims let go of the old guilt, they let go of the need to punish themselves. They then can understand that their sexuality is a good and normal part of them. Just because the first experience with sex was as a victim, they should not reject their sexuality altogether. If they ate something that made them sick, would they give up food from then on?

Q: When an adult victim discloses her past to her family, why do they turn against her, even when some of them were victims too?
A: The ones who were also victims may not be ready to face the past yet, and denial is the only way to avoid it. The mother often feels she will be, or is being, blamed. Others in the family, upon hearing the denial of the father and other victims, are anxious to believe them. After all, who wants to know that their family has been involved in sexual abuse? Sexual abuse of children in many ways involves a bigger social stigma than murder, so it is not surprising that families want to say, 'No, this isn't true.'

Q: Is it normal for a victim to feel numb and not care about anything?
A: Both are symptoms of depression. When childhood anger towards the aggressor and parents is turned inwards, it begins to be destructive. Repressed anger takes a few turns and detours and comes out in behaviours that do not resemble anger at all. Depression is one of those; self-sabotage, illness, fears, phobias and lack of confidence are some of the others.

Q: Can victims regain their self-confidence?

A: Yes. Understanding what has happened to them and where guilt belongs; letting the 'child' within finally unload anger towards the aggressor/parents; giving the 'child' information, support and love; healing negative memories with rescue scenes; turning off negative self-talk and learning assertive skills create a confident, assured and happy person.

Q: Can a female victim learn to trust men, and can a male victim learn to have a healthy relationship with women?

A: Yes. Following the steps outlined in the answer to the last question helps both male and female victims choose a partner who they will interact with in an emotionally healthy way. Victims must learn to love, like, and accept themselves before they can love, like, and accept others, and be able to *believe* that others love them too.

Q: Do victims hurt their own children?

A: According to the CIBA Foundation's report *Child Sexual Abuse within the Family* (1984), 'Sexually abused parents often abuse, physically and sexually, their own children.'

Q: How can victims accept their past and live with it?

A: Unfortunate things happen to everyone—some not as bad as sexual abuse and some worse. No one can choose what events happen to them, but they can choose how to deal with them. They can choose to say, 'Oh, this terrible thing has happened to me—I'm ruined forever' or 'Oh, this terrible thing has happened to me, but I'm not going to let it ruin the *rest* of my life.'

Q: Do the events of a victim's childhood ever fade away?

A: Yes. At first, when I spoke of my past, I would shake, perspire and feel emotionally racked. Now it is as if I am telling someone else's story. I have not forgotten it, but I have stopped hurting. Recently, one of my clients, who had a particularly horrific childhood, said to me, 'You know, whenever I have to tell you about my past again, I find it boring!' I laughed, and told her that was good evidence that the healing process was in full swing.

Q: Do victims do something to make the aggressor pick them?

A: No. They are picked simply because they are vulnerable. There is nothing children can do on their own to avoid being vulnerable—children would need adult support and information to learn assertiveness.

Q: If victims have to see their aggressors regularly (father, grandfather, etc.), how can they deal with their emotions?

A: My suggestion is that a victim tries to avoid the aggressor while in the first stages of working out the past. If she does have to see him, she should try to have as little personal interaction with him as possible. If that interaction is disturbing, later, at home alone, she can use the anger exercises (writing and pillow-bashing) to work off any anger and use the chairing exercise to let off steam orally. When the victim is gaining control over her own life, she will not feel as threatened in the presence of the aggressor.

Q: Do victims tend to feel responsible for everything happening around them?

A: This can be a very serious problem for many victims. If people carry a deep-seated guilt with them that they have never faced or understood, it becomes easy to accept further guilt or blame that has nothing to do with them, simply because of the feelings of being 'defective'. Victims have been used to assuming they are somehow to blame for negative experiences during childhood. They can spend their adult life doing the same. Learning to let go of misplaced guilt they have been carrying, replacing negative self-talk with positive attitudes, and learning some assertive skills will help them to become people in their own right. Then they will be accepting responsibility for their own mistakes but no longer doing so for others'. Victims can only change themselves and must allow others to do their own changing, leaving them to be whom they choose to be. If victims want the freedom to be themselves, they must give the same freedom to others.

14   Examples of Courage

I think it only fitting to end this book with a final word from our four main contributors: Richard, Sonja, Katy and Sylvia. They have each written a description of how life was for them before therapy, what the experience of therapy was like, how they are doing now and what their goals are for the future.

I would like to add that they are four very courageous people who I am honoured also to call my friends. Courage is doing something despite the fact that you are scared to death. We often think that courageous people feel great confidence as they go forward into battle, but not so. The courageous person goes forward, fear and all. Richard, Sonja, Katy and Sylvia are truly courageous.

Richard

I am 37 years old. I was abused by an aunt from the age of seven until the age of around twelve. Funnily enough, I didn't realise, until I spoke to Penny, just what a cunning, evil woman my aunt was.

Because of what happened to me as a child, I was unable to show or receive any form of tender affection—even a caress or a simple touch would set the alarm bells ringing. I could, however, have sex—as long as there was little cuddling or tender touching. I could see what this was doing to my wife: she naturally thought my behaviour was a reflection on her. I could also see my children needed me to be able to show them I loved them too.

I tried several times to tell my wife what happened to me as a child, but I found it very hard to come out with it. When I did manage to tell her there were tears, a lot of tears, most of them mine. I think it was mainly because of the relief I felt. I expected shock and I was ready for rejection (for at this time I still carried the guilt for what had happened); instead, I got sympathy and understanding.

I then got in touch with Penny through the Samaritans and I must admit I was dubious about talking to a therapist. I soon found that I wasn't talking to just a therapist—I was sharing my problem with someone who had gone through the same experience.

The first exercise was to get rid of the anger inside me, and I was surprised how effective an angry letter could be. I now use them in day-to-day life, not just to my aunt but to anyone or anything that has upset me. It gets rid of any anger and prevents it from coming out at the wrong time or at somebody who didn't deserve it. One little, but very important, detail in this exercise was to write down my aunt's name in small letters and not capitals—this seemed to take away her importance.

When it came to getting in touch with my 'child', it was a bit more difficult. The letters he wrote came easily—after all, he had been waiting 30 years to tell someone what had happened. It was the memories the letters brought back, the details that I had forgotten, that brought a few restless nights. But at least they were no longer on the back shelf of my memory—they were out in the open, ready to be tackled.

I think the most enjoyable exercises were the rescues. It was the child's way of getting his own back. Some of them turned out really inventive, and it surprised me how good I felt after writing them.

As well as dealing with the 'child', Penny has also taught me how to start showing and accepting emotions. I couldn't do this before, because my aunt's influence was still in control of my emotions. Now most of those strings have been cut and I am gaining full control.

It wasn't easy getting in touch with my 'child' and reliving the past, but it has been worth it. I am now able to show my wife and children I love them and, even more important, I know that they love me and are not just using me.

It may hurt you to get in touch with your 'child', but listen to him and give him the love and understanding he has waited for for so long.

Sonja

I came face to face with the realisation of having been sexually abused nineteen years after it happened. I had completely blocked it from my memory until it came out in all its questionable glory seven months ago. Actually it was a relief, because I found it tied together all the problems and feelings that I had encountered up until then which were a mystery to me.

I am now 28 years old. A year ago I had come to the conclusion that I couldn't go on feeling like I was. Basically, I hated myself, my body and men. I had reached 27 years of age and had to admit to myself that, yes, one day I would like to marry and have children, but I knew that wouldn't be possible, because of how I felt.

I had so many hang-ups about my body, about men and about the strange guilt feelings I had about my mother. These feelings were getting worse, not better, as I got older. I was depressed, not sleeping, compulsively eating, feeling inadequate and basically feeling I couldn't go on with life. Yet I didn't know why.

I had tried everything to sort myself out. Eventually I had to admit I had a problem. I wasn't even able to function properly at work and had to go off sick. I started to see a psychologist, and through his expertise this abuse all came to light a few months later. At first, all I was able to remember was my uncle coming round and touching me in a play shed from when I was eight years old. The memory didn't have a start or a finish and I didn't know then that there was a lot more to come. I was mortified. My psychologist put me in touch with Penny Parks, and I started to see her in November. I felt, even then, that I was in a large black pit and couldn't cling on to climb out. I just kept falling back down.

Over the next few months, more things gradually came to light. With all the homework I was doing—and Penny's marvellous, invaluable help—I kept remembering more and more. I remembered what I consider to be the last piece of the puzzle only a few weeks ago. I now remember the many times it happened and all that went on. It involved not only my uncle but my mother as well. I was continually being threatened, tied up, whipped, having sex and oral sex and being part of sexual acts between the two of them as well.

I can honestly say that I felt at times, especially when I had just remembered something and was completely reliving those times, that I felt like crawling into the corner of a dark room, going to sleep and never waking up. It all felt hopeless. I couldn't see how there was any light at the end of the tunnel that everyone told me about. I just felt so desperate. But, with Penny's help, I learned to reach out and find my 'inner child'. I couldn't quite grasp this at first and felt at times that, because everything felt so awful, I almost didn't want her to reach out to me. But we finally got past that part.

I found my 'inner child' and she found me. Now we help to explain to each other what is going on. My 'inner child' is at last free. She has been able to tell all that has happened, and all those feelings that have been festering away in me for nineteen years are all out now. I, as an adult, have been able to explain and give my 'child' information as we go along. I never, ever thought this would work, but it really does. It might all seem strange, but it has helped so much to cope, by using the adult–child/child–adult letter-writing techniques.

Throughout the past six months there have been many times when I almost wished I was dead. To remember all those gory details that had been festering away in me for so long seemed overwhelming. At the same time I knew I couldn't go on living the way I had been. The knowledge and information I was given by Penny and the loving support given by her set a spark alight in me to keep on pushing. It helped me really want to find a way out to feel at peace with myself at last!

I now feel that the lid has been released and that light at the end of the tunnel is well in sight. I still have some feelings and things that I need to sort out, but at least I know why I've got them and can work on that. I haven't quite finished with my 'inner child' yet!

I feel more positive now. I can look to the future and see a more 'whole', more assertive and understanding me. My inspiration all came from Penny and her therapy. I couldn't have struggled on alone—I was completely lost.

I want to be at peace with myself and function normally, and I'm nearly there. I now plan to go on and do my teacher training. There are so many outlets to look forward to in the future. Who knows what I will do? But at least, now I no longer have this burden round my neck. I'm set free, and what a relief it is!

Katy

My stepfather, John, started abusing me when I was nearly six. Then there was a gap. Later, when he and my mother married, he regularly abused me between the ages of seven and nine. John was also an alcoholic.

During the abuse he would masturbate in my presence. This he did frequently and over long periods of time. Otherwise, the abuse mostly consisted of fondling. As far as I can remember, I was never penetrated. When approached by him I became so terrified that I couldn't move or do anything. I felt completely powerless. He wasn't violent and he didn't threaten me. Each time the abuse would begin, I would think to myself, 'This is the "other world".' When I was back in the 'real world' again, I somehow blocked the incident from my mind, as if it were a dream. When I was nine, one evening he approached me when my mother was only in the next room. The two 'worlds' clashed, my anger surfaced and I shouted 'No!' He never came near me again. To my relief, six months later, he and my mother split up.

I felt terribly guilty about the abuse. Because I had been forced into arousal, I felt like an accomplice. I thought that I was evil and bad, like him. At school I felt different from other children. If I was rejected, I understood it; but if I was accepted and liked, I felt guilty. I was convinced that I was evil on the inside and that if someone liked me, then I must be deceiving them. I thought myself sly and sinister beside my 'innocent' peers. I was afraid of the opposite sex, especially later on in my teens, and avoided them as much as I could. I was mistrustful and suspicious of adults. If my mother brought a boy-friend into the house, I felt that our home was being contaminated. I had learned not to trust or respect men and, no matter how respectable they appeared to be, I felt that I could 'see through them'. All men seemed dirty to me.

I also felt that my mother was dirty for being associated with the abuser. I felt betrayed by her because she so often left me alone with him. I feel three times as angry with my mother as I do with John. I was angry with society for (like my mother) not protecting me, not taking any interest in me, not wanting to get involved. I was extremely withdrawn, so it was easy for adults to ignore me. I despised adults for demanding a respect from me which I knew they didn't deserve. I saw through their hypocrisy. When I was ten I began to release my anger in destructive activities such as stealing, trespassing and damaging property. I soon learned that I couldn't continue safely with this behaviour and so the anger was forced to stay inside. I started to punish myself, mainly by withdrawing from potential relationships. I was 'banishing' myself from people.

As a young child I recall my mother being very silent and distant. She was awkward and coy with me. There was always a sense of caution between us. She was unable to show any real affection. Mostly I was ignored. She seemed like a ghost to me—remote, unreal and intangible. Because of the lack of a bond with her I was very clingy with people who could provide something of what she couldn't. I also remember approaching strangers on the street and asking them if they could take me away with them to their home.

Mother was very ambiguous, full of contradictions. She was inconsistent and unpredictable. Sometimes she was withdrawn, pathetic and fragile, which made me feel very guilty. Mostly she was aggressive and domineering. I wasn't allowed to express anger or to confide any problems in her, because she would become hysterical. In the first case she would become violently angry, screaming and shouting at me, which would leave me feeling utterly crushed and rejected. In the second case she would dissolve into tears and become a soggy mess, so that if I was hurt I would end up having to comfort *her*! This left me with the enormous burden of protecting her from anything which might upset her. I became over-controlled in the attempt to control her hysteria. It was useless. She was extremely irritable and there was nothing I could do that wouldn't set her off screaming and criticising. The most hurtful thing of all for me was that she used me as a stand-in for men. Whenever she found a new boy-friend, I would be sent off to friends or relatives.

To cap it all, I had a sadistic uncle who specialised in humiliation. Outside the home he was ingratiating with people. But he was an inadequate and cowardly person and tried to make up for this inside the home by emotionally abusing his children, myself and anyone else when he knew he could get away with it. He would get his 'power fix' by staring and laughing at us and criticising us constantly. He always sneered and mocked. It was relentless. His behaviour, like my mother's, was exaggerated and dramatic.

I became very afraid of him and dreaded having to visit his family, which was quite often. I became increasingly self-conscious, suspicious and I couldn't bear to be looked at. Consequently I developed panic attacks on public transport and in shops where I thought that people must be spying on me and criticising my every move. I spent a lot of time alone in my bedroom to get away from 'eyes' and because I could only relax properly on my own. As long as I was in the presence of other people, I was wound up like a spring, always prepared to be let down, to be tricked. I always expected people to change and turn against me. It seemed inevitable. I developed a social phobia and withdrew more and more from people. I was particularly afraid of eating in the presence of others, especially in public places.

Because my uncle laughed at everything I did or said, I became very restricted. Despite his hysterical displays, he considered emotions to be 'stupid'. So I practised not reacting and not feeling. I contained all my feelings and acted like a robot. I couldn't afford to express myself. I felt completely trapped, boxed in from all sides. On the inside I was screaming. I had developed within me a huge stockpile of rage with nowhere to discharge it. I was full of fears which I couldn't share with anyone. I felt extremely insecure, as if I were being eaten away from the inside, crumbling to pieces.

Because of the relentless criticism from my uncle and mother, I felt 'ruined' and defective. I was very nervous and felt the need to put on a brave face in everyday life. Because of my mother's tendency to over-react, I was forced to wear a mask all the time and to pretend that everything was fine. I wore a plastic smile everywhere I went, with whoever I met. I clowned around a lot, always laughing, never taking anything seriously.

Existing in this way, on a very superficial level, kept me out of touch with the pain inside. It served as a temporary coping skill.

I experienced problems in my relationships with men. I found it difficult and sometimes impossible to have intercourse because I had vaginismus. I was pathologically jealous, which ended one of my relationships. In my present relationship my partner has been very patient and understanding with me. He gave me the time I need to overcome my jealousy. This I did by myself. It was very hard but I managed to conquer it finally and of this I am very proud.

One day, in desperation, I called the Samaritans and asked them if they knew where I could find help for my problem. They put me in touch with Penny Parks. I remember, on our first meeting, being shocked to hear her say that I was not to blame for what had happened. It was something I really needed to hear. As I heard more and more about other cases I began to feel much less of a freak and more human.

Penny set me many writing exercises. The hardest thing for me has been to face and express my anger. I had enormous resistance toward this, so much so that it was about two years later that I was able to really get into the anger exercises. My anger was connected to the feelings of victimisation and vulnerability, so I practised associating positive emotions with my anger, which freed me from this problem. I even started to enjoy it! My dreams changed dramatically. With anger on *my* side I was learning to fight off the oppressors in my dreams.

I found the parenting exercises very helpful and took to them eagerly. When Penny first suggested contacting my 'inner child', I found a photograph of myself at the age when I had first been abused. I cried for a long time because I realised that this was the child that I was blaming for what had happened. I immediately became very protective over her. I wrote letters to her and to myself at other ages. I got these other aspects of myself to write down their feelings too. Some of them even wrote to each other! This all felt very natural and I began to feel more integrated and whole.

I went through a long phase of needing to talk to my child a lot. I used a rag doll for this, which I made for myself in my own image as a six-year-old. I had missed out on so much as a child—for example, no one had ever read a story to me, so I began to read to my child. It gave me an incredible feeling inside. I found all the talking, explaining and cuddling with my child very healing. It made me less clingy with my partner. Previously, no amount of cuddling and reassurance from him would satisfy my insecurity, whereas cuddling my doll or Teddy was much more satisfactory because it was filling a part of me which he couldn't reach.

The guilt about sexual abuse has been very difficult to overcome. I wrote to my 'child' often, explaining in different ways about why she is not to blame. This was very helpful and my guilt feelings reduced considerably. But I found it hard to capture and retain that feeling. So I made a twenty-minute tape recording in which I talk directly to my child, explaining very thoroughly why she is blameless. This I listen to daily. It has helped me enormously because it is part of me now and my guilt feelings have dropped dramatically. Releasing the guilt in this way has unblocked my mind and many other feelings have surfaced of which I was previously unaware.

I still have a lot of anger to exorcise. My main problem is that I cannot work because of the anxiety I experience with people. I am still very withdrawn, spending most of my time indoors. My social phobia is the hardest, most stubborn obstacle. I hope to be eventually free from this and to lead a normal life.

Sylvia

I am the eldest daughter in a family of four children. My parents, although far from wealthy, were comfortable financially. The houses of my childhood were large, cold and somewhat forbidding for a child. My upbringing was quite strict, and a lot of emphasis was put on good manners and keeping up appearances. Father worked long hours and drank heavily. My mother was a semi-invalid and often unwell, although she worked hard and kept fairly active (a fact that added to my guilt feelings).

My childhood was surrounded in abuse. At home, I was the scapegoat and subjected to continual verbal and emotional abuse. Although not so constant, I was also often the victim of physical abuse. My mother, in particular, had some very frightening behaviour towards me, and my father would also deal me a blow when he thought I deserved it and on a few occasions really knocked me about. I also received wrenched arms, a kick or thump from my eldest brother when the mood struck him. I don't remember anyone ever standing up in my defence, and so, although I didn't like what was happening to me, I believed it was their right.

The sexual abuse started early on. There were multiple abusers, the main one being my uncle who for some years lived next to us. He abused me from the age of three (that is my earliest recollection) until I was able to put a stop to it in my teens. The most horrific time was somewhere been the ages of five and seven when he subjected me to torture and humiliating experiences which also involved his girl-friend. I began to feel it was my lot in life to be abused.

Wherever I went, whatever I did, it seemed like there was someone waiting to put his hand down my panties. I know now that those who take advantage of children watch and recognise the signs of need in their victims. But at the time I thought I was just bad and that it had been ordained that I was there to be of use to everyone else. In fact, at one time I even doubted my birth and believed I was just an object manufactured for this purpose. To say my childhood was unhappy is probably an understatement. I had a pain deep inside me all the time—the pain of sadness, a mourning for something.

My family made me feel bad, dirty, stupid, ugly and smelly, calling me those names often. I felt less than the dog. If anything went wrong it was my fault; if I laughed it was too loud; if I cried it was wrong, I was ungrateful and looked silly; if I expressed an opinion it was stupid; if I made a friend there was always something wrong about them. I quickly learned not to think, feel or show any emotion. I became as emotive and spontaneous as an old piece of furniture.

I spent a lot of my childhood frightened. I had all sorts of fears, but particularly I was afraid of my mother. I'd lie in bed in the mornings, feeling the atmosphere in the house. Instinctively, I'd know if she were in a bad mood and be afraid to get up because I would bear the brunt of her mood.

I could never tell anyone about why I was unhappy. I didn't really know the sort of things that were happening to me were wrong, but anyway I had learned not to communicate my feelings, fears or opinions. If I dared to think someone might really like me, I would try to plead with them in thought, willing them to help me. But, of course, no one heard. I used to watch other children playing and laughing. I rarely joined in—my thoughts were too full of pain. I knew I was different to them in some way and was very aware I would look silly and ugly.

It is hard to explain my feelings as a child—perhaps total hopelessness and submission. I couldn't laugh or cry properly. I was in mourning and never felt wanted or accepted. I felt I was in a box, my eyes being holes to look out of. I felt continually on show, being watched—even if there was no one around. When I met an abuser, it felt as though it had been arranged. Like when I was on holiday with a friend's family. I went alone to look at the sea and a man came up whose surname was the same as my friend's. He abused me throughout the holiday. I somehow thought it was OK because of the name. I didn't know about coincidence then. This sort of thing happened regularly.

Sometime in my early teens my mother was forced, by my aunt, into the position where she had to accuse me of 'letting my uncle do dirty things to me'. Her aggressive and accusing manner prevented me from admitting anything. I think she already knew the truth but felt obligated to put on a performance of asking me, just to keep up appearances. During that discourse she spat names at me—'slut', 'whore', 'prostitute'. She said only evil, dirty girls let men do those things to them. (I often wonder what would have happened had I actually admitted it!) Not only did I already own the negative labels I had heard all my life (bad, ugly, smelly) but now I knew I was also evil, dirty and a slut.

I began to take ridiculous risks, did stupid things and became that slut. I didn't care what happened to me. I think I was about fourteen when I started cutting myself. I didn't know why or even that I was doing it, but I caught sight of myself in the bathroom mirror cutting slits into my chest with my father's razor-blade. Fortunately, I didn't do any permanent damage and this stage didn't last long, but it left me convinced that I was mad. In fact, until recently I have carried that secret as safely as the abuse, in case someone would want to lock me up in a mental home.

I married at nineteen. I think I felt I would then be an 'adult' and out of my parents' power. I believed a wedding-ring would save me from further sexual abuse. At first it was OK, but then my husband seemed to take over from my parents. He was verbally abusive and very dominant. I returned to my passive, obedient self and became his doormat. On the rare occasions I asserted myself, he would fly off the handle and become physically abusive. Perhaps because of my faith at that time, I believed that, even when I knew he was wrong, he was right. My self-respect took a further beating.

By the time I was thirty, we had children, were badly in debt and I was going downhill fast. I had struggled all my life to keep as near to normality as possible, but the strain of keeping myself together was overwhelming. I had believed I would make a good mother and give the children all the love and security I lacked, but I now felt I had failed. Every time I shouted at them thoughtlessly, I would pile great heaps of guilt on myself. This just added to the shame of my past.

The insecurity of our financial position, a relationship in shambles, and the feelings of responsibility were just too much to cope with. If I couldn't make life work for me, I'd rather be dead. I was convinced that the children would be better off with a proper mother. Slipping further away from normality, I began to drink heavily and had all sorts of phobias and fears. Sometimes I'd sit all day in the armchair, alternating between staring into space, sleeping, drinking or eating. I'd ignore the phone ringing or be too afraid to answer it. If we went out for the evening, I'd panic and have to leave. I'd only go out in the car, for I couldn't even walk out into my village. These and other behaviours caused more friction with my husband, who told me to pull myself together. But I couldn't—I really couldn't—all my fight had gone.

I was then referred to a family psychiatrist. Unfortunately, he didn't consider child sexual abuse had any bearing on a woman of my age, so I could only tell him the barest details. He appeared to consider me a 'bored housewife with nothing better to think about', and more or less told me to go home and find something to do. I was devastated. He had been my last resort. It had taken every ounce of strength I had to go and admit I needed help and I had believed at last someone was going to help me. I went away feeling that if this learned man said there was nothing wrong with me, and I knew I couldn't help it, then it was now time to die. It was a calm feeling, once the hurt had gone. It was one of the few decisions I had ever made in my life. It was a promise to myself for myself. I would pick my time carefully so I didn't mess it up.

A person came into my life about that time, to whom I will be eternally grateful. She had heard Penny Parks speak and suggested that we phone her to see if she could see me. I was a while making up my mind, but I finally decided that it couldn't hurt any more than the psychiatrist, yet I didn't believe deep down that there was much point. However, I thought it would be better to be seen as co-operating than to make waves by refusing. My resolve to die however was not changed. But I didn't know I was about to meet an angel, with the love and knowledge to make me begin to feel a person.

An appointment was made, and as we drove I felt like a humiliated little puppy-dog. I was weighed down with shame and felt totally defeated. As we walked up the path, the door was opened by an attractive, smiling woman. She welcomed us in an American accent as though she had known us for years. Seated inside, my fears of having to lie on a couch were quickly eased. It was a very friendly, informal atmosphere.

I imagine I was very hard work on that first interview. I didn't dare to look up, I didn't want to talk, I only answered questions put directly to me. Penny told us something of her past, and it struck me by what she was saying (the little I was able to take in) that finally here was someone who knew how I felt. The bombshell came when, nearing the end of the session, she asked about the next appointment. I had been naïve enough to think it would be a one-off. They were waiting for me to make a decision, not realising how difficult decisions were for me. Finally, I mumbled something in agreement. She loaded me with lots of literature and we left. On the way home it occurred to me that this woman seemed genuine in her interest in me and in her concern for other victims of past abuse. If anyone could help me, it would be her.

The first couple of months of therapy were very hard for me.

I am not very verbal and found it hard to put my thoughts into words. I think Penny recognised this, plus her methods made it easier for me. Her calm acceptance and matter-of-fact attitude were right—I couldn't have handled great rushes of sympathy or hard, pushy therapy. The knowledge that she too had been abused made me feel less of a freak. Seeing how she had managed total recovery by the methods she was now teaching me gave me an incentive. I realised it was possible for one to transform from a damaged victim into a completely whole human being. I now had a reason to live, a reason to fight my past and work hard on my recovery.

To say that I became an obedient slave to Penny and to the homework exercises would be taking it too far, but such was my passion to get well quickly that I eagerly awaited the homework and was willing to try anything that she would throw in my direction—including some of the exercises which to me at first seemed really strange, bordering on fantasy.

It is hard now to remember exactly in what order I did my homework exercises, but I think anger letters were among the first. In fact it took many months for me to accept that I had a right to be angry. It was a strange new concept that I could be angry for myself. I had buried anger so deep that I didn't recognise that I had any. I also tried the pillow-bashing exercises and cuddling a soft toy. But I believe that the exercise which has been of the most help to me was the very one that I was the most sceptical about.

Penny spoke a lot about the 'inner child', about how the hurting 'child' (myself as a child) rules and governs our present. To be honest, I didn't really understand what she was talking about at first. It seemed very fanciful and quite a good excuse for one's present-day behaviours. She explained that a child when faced with a traumatic experience will stop growing emotionally and stay at that level of emotional development. While outwardly the child grows to become an adult, the emotional development is frozen. This did in fact make some sense to me and I could identify with it. But when she suggested that I might start making contact with the 'child', I nearly laughed out loud. However, as I have already said, I was willing to try anything. My assignment for that week was to write to the 'child' telling her that I understood how she felt and that she wasn't alone now—that she was a sweet, nice little girl and that I was here to support and comfort her. I was to learn to love my child.

Well, no one had ever loved me as a child and the information that I had been given by my family about her was far from good, so it wasn't likely that I could love her. So, at first it seemed an impossible task. I didn't even like my memories of her. I believe I made several attempts at it. Penny even suggested I get a photo of myself as a child and look at it while writing. Quite frankly that didn't help at first, because I'd always thought of myself as ugly and unlovable. But after a while I managed to detach my negative thoughts about her looks and see her as just a little girl. (When writing to my 'child' now I have no need for a picture of her. It is more of a spiritual thing—I am communicating with something deep inside me or my subconscious.)

Writing to the 'child' and having her write back to me was very wooden at first—I didn't believe in it at all. When I wrote to her, I just wrote down more or less what Penny had suggested. When she wrote back to me it was a conscious effort from my memory. I then had to again write back and thank her for sharing with me and comfort her. I wonder if this was the turning point? The 'child' must have heard and understood what I was saying and started to learn to trust me.

At that stage, after writing woodenly to my 'child', asking her to express her feelings about a certain event, she seemed to take over. I wasn't really aware of what she was writing. I didn't have to keep stopping and wondering what to write next. The memories and emotions just flowed on to the paper from somewhere in my subconscious. She had become real. Then, as I looked back over the piece I had just written, I felt somewhat strange for the writing had deteriorated and looked like a child's. The spelling and sentence construction were like those of a child, and yet I knew I had just written it. I have since learned that it is not uncommon for this to happen, although it doesn't happen every time my 'child' writes back to me.

I had surface memories of the abuse of my childhood, but I was aware of what I can only describe as blank spaces and fogs that I knew held memories which were too painful to surface. My 'child' helped me to open some of these memories up. One may wonder why I should want to dig up memories which my mind had been so successful in hiding. To be honest, for a time, I felt this way myself. Now I can see that memories so well hidden are damaged, hurt memories which, unless brought to the surface and dealt with, cause awful problems for the present. I also found that whereas I (the adult) might only have a dark, foggy recollection of a memory, my 'child', when asked to write to me expressing her feelings of the event, could remember so much more.

I am not suggesting that these were easy times—the revelations that came from the 'child' were often extremely alarming and even frightening. I found it difficult to deal with what she told me, and would relive the awful experiences again and again in my mind. Sometimes I would not want to accept what she told me—particularly the occasions with my uncle and his girl-friend. I wanted to pretend that I still couldn't remember and in this way convince myself that it didn't happen.

I believe a lot of healing comes when I write back to the 'child' pointing out that she was only a little girl and in no way responsible. That she was a sweet, innocent little thing and that it was the adults around her that were at fault. I praise and thank her for being brave enough to tell me. I build her self-esteem and confidence and in effect give her the affection she so desperately needed as a child. As the 'child' begins to accept and believe what I tell her, the hold and hurt of that particular memory fades. She no longer feels she is guilty, her shame recedes and another step in her emotional growth is achieved.

The more my 'child' confides in me, the more respect I have for her and the easier I find it to love her, and so the easier it becomes to love and forgive myself. I can see that the 'child' wasn't responsible and therefore I was not responsible. I am then able to unload a lot of guilt and shame. Getting to know my 'child' has been one of the greatest gifts I have experienced —it has brought me countless blessings. I would liken getting to know the 'child', and reviving forgotten memories and emotions, to having surgery: the long-term benefits are well worth the short-term pain.

I know my 'child' has a lot more to share with me, and when

the time is right for her I will be more than willing to listen and support her, realising that this will also be of benefit to the adult me. I no longer laugh when the 'inner child' is mentioned—she is the living, hurt part of my subconscious, needing love and acceptance, but quite capable, unless educated, of ruining my present and future.

My therapy sessions became a very important part of my life. It seems strange, now, that I was so reluctant at first. Somehow, without my realising it, they became to mean so much to me. When I started I was full of hopelessness, shame, phobias, panics, etc. I could hear the sound of my dead mother's voice wherever I went. Gradually, almost unperceived, these things lost their hold on me. So, if I had a reputation, I would stake it on the exercises that Penny gave me to use. Her insistence that I was blameless, her acceptance and understanding of me, along with my desire to be well, and the exercises were the remedy to my problems.

Penny will take no credit for herself concerning a client's recovery—she says a client does all the work. In some ways this is true, but I thank God for Penny. If she had not been there and willing to give information and example, I would have had no chance of recovery. I pray that many victims will read her book, learn and use the techniques described, and experience a full life as a result.

I went through many stages during therapy. Mostly I was encouraged and eager to go on, but there were times when I would feel depressed and totally fed-up even with the words 'child abuse'. The flashbacks and opening of closed memories were very difficult to deal with, as were the times I felt I had failed when old behaviours would rear their heads and depression would set in. Penny says you take two steps forward and one step back, and I found this to be very true. Mind you, it is a splendid feeling when you find the one step back is becoming less frequent.

There are still a few battles to be conquered for me, one of which is not being able to speak out—to say what I am thinking or feeling *at the time I am experiencing it.* Many times I go home from a session still troubled, simply because I have not shared what was going on in my mind. This is a lacking in me, where my 'child' takes over, not in the therapist who gives me opportunity to speak. Another problem that I found was that there was no one I was able to share with between sessions, and at times I desperately needed the support of another. I would advise anyone thinking of embarking on these sorts of exercises, particularly when reliving painful memories, to have someone they can share with—a good friend or partner. Remembering can be mind-blowing and terrifying, and you may need a lot of support at the time these memories surface. It may be an idea to prepare your friend or partner that this may happen. There were many times I felt like giving up, but I am grateful that I have a survival instinct and a great desire to get well to keep me going even though I had no one to share with.

Although I put a stop to the abuse by my uncle in my teens, I believe that I was sexually and emotionally abused right into my early thirties. This may seem unbelievable as I was an 'adult' and a free-thinking person, and it may seem I am making excuses for my behaviour. However, in reality I was still that little abused 'child', functioning on the knowledge and experience that she had. She had no way of protecting herself from the will of others and was at the mercy of anyone who would take advantage. She could not trust, believe herself acceptable, realise she had rights, bear physical contact or dare hope for happiness. She felt doomed to die at her own hand.

Now, approximately one year into therapy, I feel alive and I am looking forward to a future. I have learned to be assertive when I choose, to consider my own happiness as well as the wishes of others. I have revived emotions that I had buried deep. My marriage is more bearable and, because I am taking a more assertive role, we are no longer in debt. I am more relaxed with my children, and in fact I am a different person.

I know that there are still parts of me that I will have to work on, and that my 'child' still has hurts that need healing. I, like everyone else, will have to face unhappy times in the future, but I am convinced that I now have the tools (exercises) and information to deal with them. I can make my life as rich as I choose. I am no longer at the mercy of others—I am growing up. My plans for the future are to enjoy as much of my life as I can, and to pass on the priceless information that I have learned so that others can learn to respect themselves and live a full life.

Sexual Abuse

It's been over for 30 years.
I've come a long way—
No more nightmares;
No more shakes, sweating or panic
When I talk about it.

I've learned to stop blaming myself.
I've stopped hating my mother
For not saving me.
Anger and bitterness towards my stepfather,
And the five others,
Have slowly ebbed away.

I have finally chosen a partner
Who is loving.
No longer sabotaging my happiness
With people and problems,
To pay for a debt that I never owed.
I don't feel defective any longer.

But, still, when I hear the stories
Of others like me, I cry.
There seems to be a terrible grief inside.
A howling cry that would finish me
If I let it out.
Grief for innocence and freedom
I never knew as a child.
Grief for the others, not as lucky as I,
Whose loss may consume them.

Penny Parks

Summary

There is no one answer for anyone's problems, nor any one book with all the answers. In this book, you have found a few keys to open doors formerly closed to you. Use the following Book List to continue this process.

Most victims understand the feeling of living in only a small part of themselves—the feeling that there are dark, forbidding rooms that one must not go into. By learning about yourself and applying that knowledge to change your attitudes and behaviour, you can unlock and clear out those forbidding rooms. Each new bit of applied knowledge becomes something lovely to decorate your new rooms with. You will begin to feel like you are living in all your rooms rather than just the secret, closed-off rooms which have been sparsely furnished and dimly lit. (That is to say, they contained little information or applied knowledge.) You now have the chance to create a lovely, welcoming home within, so *learn* and *apply* that knowledge to *change* negative attitudes and behaviours.

Book List

Betrayal of Innocence: Incest and Its Devastation, Susan Forward and Craig Buck (Penguin, 1981). A good overview of the subject of sexual abuse. Contains valuable information that can be written to the 'child'.

The Last Taboo: Sexual Abuse of Children, Gay Search (Penguin, 1988). Another book with a good overview of the subject. It also contains insightful information from people working directly with victims and with abusers. More valuable information to help the 'child' understand what happened to her and why.

Staying OK, Amy and Thomas Harris (Pan, 1986). A good book to help sort out the three 'voices'—'damaged Parent', 'damaged Child' and 'Adult'. One must be able to recognise these three 'voices' before one can put the 'adult' in charge of damaging self-talk.

Born to Win: Transactional Analysis with Gestalt experiments, Muriel James and Dorothy Jongeward (Addison-Wesley, 1971). A thorough explanation of the three 'voices' (transactional analysis), the games we play when ruled by the damaged voices, a clear explanation of what it is like for the 'adult' voice to be in executive control and useful exercises. A much more in-depth book than *Staying OK*.

A Woman in Your Own Right, Anne Dickson (Quartet, 1982). A book about assertiveness, with good examples of the personality types for 'passive', 'aggressive' and 'assertive' behaviour. It will help you assess which side you err on most often and provide a positive 'adult' (assertive) behaviour example to follow.

When I Say No, I Feel Guilty, Manuel J. Smith (Bantam, 1976). Another assertiveness book. This one provides good dialogue for your 'adult' voice to learn. Most victims have very weak and ineffective 'adult' (assertive) voices. *A Woman In Your*

Own Right will show you proper behaviour; *When I Say No, I Feel Guilty* will provide you with the actual words you can use.

Assert Yourself: a Self-assertiveness Programme for Men and Women, Gael Lindenfield (Thorsons, 1987). Written in a personal and friendly style. Easy to read and simply explained, with helpful exercises for either groups or individuals.

Women Who Love Too Much, Robin Norwood (Arrow, 1976). An excellent book explaining why a person damaged in childhood often ends up with a damaged partner. Riveting material, but a bit thin when it comes to how to overcome the problems discussed.

Treat Yourself to Sex: a Guide to Good Loving, Paul Brown and Carolyn Foulder (Penguin, 1979). A straightforward look at a delicate subject—good practical information. For victims, a good example of a healthy attitude towards sex.

Questions of Sex, The Diagram Group (New English Library, 1989). An excellent book to clarify the information victims have about sexual and personal subjects. A source of answers to big or niggling questions.

The Mirror Within: a New Look at Sexuality, Anne Dickson (Quartet, 1985). A book about female sexuality and body-image. Simply written and easy to understand, with useful exercises.

Men and Sex, Bernie Zilbergeld (Fontana, 1980). Explodes myths about, and explains reasons for, male sexual problems. Written in a down-to-earth manner, with self-help exercises.

Keeping Safe: a Practical Guide to Talking with Children, Michele Elliott (New English Library, 1988). An easy-to-understand book written to help parents equip their children with information about avoiding sexual abuse, *without* discussing sex. Clever accomplishment—excellent book.

No More Secrets: Protecting Your Child from Sexual Assault, Caren Adams and Jennifer Fay (Impact Publishers (US), 1983). Valuable information for parents who need help to equip their children with prevention skills (including games to play that reinforce prevention ideas) and for parents who need help to deal with children who have already been abused. Easy to read, with chapters arranged so that parents with particular interests can quickly locate the sections they need. A small but powerful book.

Helping Agencies

Childhood Sexual Abuse Centre (Founder: Penny Parks)
29 Lower Brook Street, Ipswich, Suffolk, IP4 1AQ
  The Centre offers Parks Inner Child Therapy (PICT) counselling and hypnotherapy. Counselling is available to male and female victims (age seventeen and above), to mothers and siblings of victims and to potential abusers (those who are afraid that they may abuse). Male or female counsellors work with clients who were either sexually, physically or emotionally abused. PICT training courses are available and workshops on sexual abuse or speakers can be booked.

Breakthrough Training Programmes
(Executive Director: Vera Diamond)
101 Harley Street, London W1N 1DF (071-486 1568)
  Offering international training programmes for professionals (including statutory agencies) who work with adults, children and/or abusers in the sexual abuse field.

National Society for the Prevention of Cruelty to Children (NSPCC)
67 Saffron Hill, London EC1N 8RS (071-404 4447 or 071-242 1626)
  Other offices are listed in local phone books.

The Royal Scottish Society for the Prevention of Cruelty to Children (RSSPCC)
Melville House, 41 Polwarth Terrace, Edinburgh EH11 1NU (031-337 8530 or 031-337 8539)

OPUS (Organisation for Parents under Stress)
106 Godstone Road, Whyteleafe, Surrey CR3 0EB (071-263 5672 or 081-645 0469)

Rape Crisis Centre
PO Box 69, London WC1X 9NJ

071-837 1600 (London)
041-221 8448 (Scotland)
0222 733929 (Wales—Incest Survivors Helpline)

If Rape Crisis Centres cannot offer counselling, they can usually refer you to any local incest survivor groups.

Kidscape (Founder: Michele Elliott)
World Trade Centre, Europe House,
London E1 9AA (071-488 0488)
Kidscape offers programmes in preventing child abuse. Schools wishing to use the Kidscape programme or parents wanting a free leaflet on how to protect their children should send a large stamped addressed envelope to the address above.

Gracewell Clinic (Director: Ray Wire)
25-29 Park Road, Moseley,
Birmingham B13 8AH (021-442 4994)
A residential treatment centre for abusers.